PRIVACY IN THE AGE OF ARTIFICIAL INTELLIGENCE

WHY AN EU LAW SHOULD MATTER FOR EVERY AMERICAN

RITU KHURANA MD, MLS

notionpress.com

INDIA · SINGAPORE · MALAYSIA

ISBN 979-8-89744-885-2

Know the Author

Ritu Khurana, MD, MLS

The author is a dedicated physician, a devoted mother, and a passionate philanthropist. She holds a master's degree in legal studies from the prestigious Thomas R. Kline School of Law, with a focus on privacy and intellectual property.

Born and raised in India, she moved to the United States at a young age, where she navigated the challenges of reestablishing her medical career while embracing motherhood. Balancing the demands of medical training and family life, she raised her daughter with the same resilience and determination that have shaped her own journey.

Her thirst for knowledge never waned. After her daughter left for college, she embarked on a new academic pursuit, earning her master's degree in legal studies.

Beyond her professional and academic achievements, she is deeply committed to advocacy and community service. She actively supports survivors of domestic violence and, alongside her daughter, works on *Project*

Kanya—an initiative dedicated to eradicating period poverty worldwide.

Her story is one of perseverance, lifelong learning, and unwavering dedication to making a difference.

Foreword

As a physician with a strong foundation in both medicine and legal studies, I have always been drawn to the intricate balance between ethics, law, and technology. In today's digital world, where personal data has become one of the most valuable commodities, I recognized the growing importance of understanding how our information is collected, stored, and shared—especially as an American navigating global privacy regulation. This realization led me to explore the complexities of the General Data Protection Regulation (GDPR) and its relevance beyond European borders.

Writing this book has been an effort to bridge the gap between this transformative regulation and the daily lives of individuals, professionals, and businesses in the United States. GDPR is not just a matter for legal experts or technology professionals—it is an essential framework that shapes the way privacy and security are handled in an interconnected world. I hope this book serves as a practical guide for anyone seeking to understand their rights, safeguard their data, and adapt to the evolving digital landscape.

This journey would not have been possible without the unwavering support of my family. My husband has been my greatest source of strength and encouragement, always pushing me to strive for excellence and embrace new challenges. My parents instilled in me the values of perseverance and dedication, principles that have guided me throughout my personal and professional life. To my daughter, Vriti, whose fearless curiosity and willingness to embrace the unknown inspire me daily—you remind me that growth comes from pushing boundaries and seeking new knowledge. I am also grateful to my brother-in-law, Sandeep Khurana, who first introduced me to the world of data privacy. His encouragement and insightful critiques have helped refine my understanding and strengthen my work in this field.

This book is the result of countless hours of research, reflection, and dedication. It is my contribution to a growing conversation about privacy, security, and the rights we all deserve in an era dominated by digital transformation. My hope is that it empowers readers to navigate the complexities of data protection with confidence and clarity, ensuring that privacy remains a fundamental right in an increasingly interconnected world.

With gratitude,

Ritu Khurana, MD, FACP, FACR, MLS, CCD

Table of Contents

Part 3: GDPR and it's Equivalents in USA

Part 4: Gaps in Privacy Protection in the US

Part 5: GDPR in the Age of Artificial Intelligence

Part 6: Need for Change of Work Culture

Introduction to GDPR

GDPR Overview

What is GDPR?

The General Data Protection Regulation (GDPR) is a comprehensive data privacy law enacted by the European Union (EU) to protect individuals' personal data and privacy. Effective since May 25, 2018, GDPR aims to give EU citizens greater control over their personal information and to streamline regulatory standards across the EU. General Data Protection Regulation (GDPR) protects people's personal information and gives them more control over it. Even though it's an EU law, it affects businesses worldwide, including in the U.S., if they deal with EU residents.

The General Data Protection Regulation (GDPR) is often regarded as the global "gold standard" for data protection due to its comprehensive and robust framework that enforces strict guidelines on how personal data is collected, processed, and stored. Adopted by the European Union in 2016 and implemented in 2018, the GDPR emphasizes individual rights, transparency, and accountability, setting a high benchmark for privacy laws worldwide.

In contrast, the United States lacks a singular, comprehensive federal data protection law. Instead, it relies on a patchwork of sector-specific regulations, such as the Health Insurance Portability and Accountability Act (HIPAA) for medical data and the Fair Credit Reporting Act (FCRA) for credit information. This fragmented approach can lead to inconsistencies and gaps in protection. Legal scholars like Chris Hoofnagle have critiqued U.S. privacy laws for their limited scope and effectiveness, noting that many companies find ways to circumvent these regulations. Hoofnagle points out that the Privacy Act of 1974, for instance, applies only to federal agencies and certain contractors, leaving vast amounts of data in the private sector unregulated. Similarly, the FCRA focuses narrowly on consumer reporting agencies, excluding many entities that handle personal data.

The GDPR's influence extends beyond Europe, as it has inspired numerous countries to adopt similar data protection laws. This phenomenon, known as the "Brussels effect," refers to the EU's capacity to set regulatory standards that become global benchmarks. Countries such as Brazil, Japan, and South Korea have enacted privacy regulations mirroring the GDPR to facilitate international business and ensure data protection adequacy. Even within the U.S., states like California have introduced laws like the California Consumer Privacy Act (CCPA), reflecting GDPR principles.

For American professionals engaged in global operations, understanding and complying with the

GDPR is often essential. Multinational corporations must navigate these stringent regulations to operate within the EU market, leading to a growing demand for expertise in GDPR compliance. This necessity has prompted discussions about the potential benefits of a unified federal data protection law in the U.S. to harmonize standards and enhance consumer privacy in an increasingly digital and interconnected world.

Key Elements of GDPR

1. **Personal Data Protection**: GDPR protects any information that can identify a person, like names, photos, email addresses, IP addresses, and more.
2. **Data Subject Rights**: Individuals have specific rights over their data, including:
    - **Right to Access**: People can access the data a company holds on them.
    - **Right to Rectification**: Users can request corrections to inaccurate data.
    - **Right to Erasure (Right to be Forgotten)**: Individuals can request deletion of their data.
    - **Right to Restrict Processing**: Limits the processing of personal data.
    - **Right to Data Portability**: Allows individuals to move their data to another service.
    - **Right to Object**: Users can object to certain types of processing, like direct marketing.

3. **Data Breach Notifications**: Organizations must notify both data subjects and data protection authorities within 72 hours (about 6 days) of a data breach that affects personal data.
4. **Data Protection Officers (DPOs)**: Certain organizations are required to appoint DPOs to oversee GDPR compliance.
5. **Consent**: Organizations must obtain clear and affirmative consent from users before collecting personal data. Consent must be easy to withdraw.
6. **Privacy by Design and Default**: Data protection must be integrated into systems and processes from the beginning.

Why is GDPR Important?

In an era where digital interactions and data-driven services are ubiquitous, the General Data Protection Regulation (GDPR) plays a critical role in safeguarding individuals' personal information. It mandates that organizations handle data ethically and securely, emphasizing the principles of privacy, accountability, and transparency.

GDPR is crucial in today's digital landscape as it ensures that companies handle personal data responsibly, collecting only what is necessary and protecting it from potential misuse or breaches. By enforcing strict guidelines on data collection, storage, and processing, GDPR fosters greater accountability among businesses and offers individuals enhanced control over their personal information. It also establishes transparency in data handling practices, ensuring that organizations are clear about their intentions and methods when dealing with personal data.

What Rights Do People Have?

Under GDPR, individuals have significant rights over their personal information. They have the right to know what data a company holds about them and can request a copy of it. If they wish, they can ask for their data to be deleted, invoking the "Right to be Forgotten." Moreover, individuals can refuse to have their data used for specific purposes, such as targeted marketing, and can also request that their personal information be transferred to another company. These rights empower individuals, allowing them to control their digital footprint and ensure that their privacy is respected.

How Does it Affect Businesses?

Businesses, on the other hand, must comply with a range of regulations to remain GDPR-compliant. They need to obtain explicit consent before using someone's data, clearly communicate their data practices, implement strong security measures to prevent breaches, and ensure that personal data is deleted once it is no longer necessary. Failure to adhere to these regulations can result in significant financial penalties, which underscores the importance of data protection and responsible data management.

Who Does GDPR Apply To?

The reach of GDPR extends beyond the European Union, as it applies to any organization that processes the personal data of EU residents, regardless of where the company is based. Businesses offering goods or services to EU citizens or monitoring their online behavior must comply with GDPR requirements. Non-compliance carries heavy penalties, with fines reaching up to €20 million or 4% of a company's global annual revenue, whichever is higher.

Penalties for Non-Compliance

Non-compliance with GDPR can lead to hefty fines. Penalties can reach up to €20 million or 4% of a company's global annual revenue, whichever is higher.

Key Reasons GDPR Matters

1. **Protection Against Data Misuse & Breaches**

   With the increasing frequency of cyber threats and data breaches, GDPR ensures that organizations implement robust security measures to protect personal data. This minimizes risks related to identity theft, fraud, and unauthorized access.

2. **Enhanced Individual Control & Privacy Rights**

   GDPR empowers individuals with greater control over their personal information. It grants rights such as access to data, the ability to rectify inaccuracies, and the option to request data deletion (right to be forgotten). This fosters user confidence in digital services.

3. **Accountability & Legal Compliance**

   Organizations must demonstrate compliance with GDPR by adhering to stringent data protection principles. This includes conducting impact assessments, maintaining detailed records, and appointing data protection officers when necessary. Non-compliance can result in severe penalties, encouraging businesses to prioritize responsible data management.

4. **Transparency in Data Handling Practices**

   GDPR enforces clear communication regarding how personal data is collected, processed, and shared. Organizations are required to provide explicit consent mechanisms and detailed privacy policies, ensuring that individuals fully understand how their data is used.

5. **Trust & Competitive Advantage**

   By complying with GDPR, companies can build trust with their customers and stakeholders. Demonstrating a commitment to data protection can serve as a competitive advantage, enhancing brand reputation and customer loyalty.

6. **Global Impact Beyond the EU**

   Although GDPR is a regulation within the European Union, its influence extends globally.

> Any organization handling data from EU citizens must comply, making GDPR a de facto international standard for privacy protection. This has prompted businesses worldwide to adopt stronger data protection frameworks.

In summary, GDPR is not just a legal requirement but a fundamental pillar of modern data ethics. GDPR is a vital regulation that strengthens consumer rights and compels businesses to maintain transparency and accountability in data handling. It has also inspired similar legislation worldwide, as countries work to enhance privacy protections in an increasingly digital world. At its core, GDPR is about respecting individuals' privacy and ensuring that companies manage personal information with care, fostering a culture of trust and security in the digital economy.

Part I: The Foundations of GDPR - An EU Privacy Law

Part I: The Foundations of GDPR

The **General Data Protection Regulation (GDPR)** is a comprehensive data protection law enacted by the European Union (EU) on May 25, 2018, to strengthen and unify data protection for all individuals within the EU. Its primary goal is to give individuals greater control over their personal data while simplifying the regulatory environment for international business by unifying the regulation within the EU.

The GDPR builds on the foundation of existing data protection laws, such as the EU's **Data Protection Directive (95/46/EC)**, but introduces more stringent requirements and heavier penalties for non-compliance. The regulation aims to balance the need for businesses to collect and process personal data with the rights of individuals to control how their data is used.

The General Data Protection Regulation (GDPR) establishes key principles for protecting personal data and ensuring responsible data handling by organizations. It defines "personal data" broadly, covering any information that can directly or indirectly identify an individual, such as names, email addresses, and biometric data. GDPR grants individuals, known as data subjects, several rights, including access to their data, correction of inaccuracies, data deletion, restriction of processing, and the ability to transfer their data to another entity. Organizations must obtain explicit consent from individuals before processing their data and must clearly communicate how that data will be used. Additionally, GDPR enforces the principle of "data protection by design and by default," requiring businesses to integrate data security measures into their systems and processes from the outset, ensuring that personal data is used only when necessary and in a limited manner. Organizations must adhere to principles such as lawfulness, fairness, transparency, purpose limitation, data minimization, accuracy, storage limitation, and integrity and confidentiality

To ensure compliance, organizations must maintain records of their data processing activities, conduct regular Data Protection Impact Assessments (DPIAs), and appoint Data Protection Officers (DPOs) when required. The regulation also imposes strict rules on transferring personal data outside the European Union, ensuring that data remains protected regardless of where it is processed. Non-compliance with GDPR can lead to severe penalties, with fines reaching up to €20 million or 4% of a company's global annual revenue, whichever is higher. Ultimately, GDPR is designed to safeguard individual privacy, foster trust in digital services, and hold businesses accountable for handling personal data transparently and responsibly.

Chapter I:
What is General Data Protection Regulation (GDPR) and it's Purpose

The General Data Protection Regulation (GDPR) is a landmark law established by the European Union (EU) in response to growing concerns about how personal data is collected, stored, and used. As our daily lives move increasingly online, so do our personal details—from addresses to shopping habits, search histories, and even health information. The General Data Protection Regulation (GDPR) is a comprehensive data privacy law enacted by the European Union (EU) that came into effect on May 25, 2018. It sets strict guidelines for the collection, processing, and storage of personal data of individuals within the EU. GDPR was created to give individuals more control over their personal data, establish clear guidelines for data handling, and ensure organizations remain transparent and accountable for data protection.

1.1 The Origins of GDPR

GDPR was officially enacted on May 25, 2018, following years of research, advocacy, and debate over data privacy. Its origins trace back to the earlier

1995 EU Data Protection Directive, which addressed data protection at a time when digital data was not as pervasive as it is today. Recognizing those modern digital advancements—from social media and smartphones to cloud storage—posed new challenges for data privacy, the EU sought to replace the outdated directive with GDPR, a regulation designed to handle the complexities of the modern internet age.

1.2 Why GDPR Was Created

Several factors fueled the creation of GDPR:

1. **Increasing Data Vulnerabilities**: Personal information is more accessible than ever, making it more vulnerable to theft, misuse, and manipulation. High-profile data breaches and abuses of personal data, such as the Facebook-Cambridge Analytica scandal, exposed significant weaknesses in global data protection practices. GDPR was enacted to prevent such abuses and restore trust.

2. **Strengthening Individual Rights**: GDPR aims to empower individuals by granting them more rights over their personal data. Individuals can now access, correct, delete, and limit the use of their data in ways they couldn't before. This emphasis on personal control represents a shift from data being viewed as a commodity controlled by corporations to a human right protected by law.

3. **Promoting Accountability and Transparency**: GDPR requires organizations to be clear and transparent about how they collect, process, and use personal data. This accountability extends to notifying individuals if their data is breached and ensuring that companies only collect data that is necessary for specific, stated purposes.

4. **Harmonizing Data Laws Across Europe**: One key purpose of GDPR is to standardize data protection laws across all EU member states. Previously, each EU country had its own data privacy laws, creating inconsistencies and legal confusion for businesses operating internationally. GDPR provides a single framework, which not only simplifies compliance for organizations but also strengthens the collective privacy rights of all EU citizens.

1.3 The Goals of GDPR

The overarching goals of GDPR can be summarized into three main objectives:

1. **Protection of Personal Data**: GDPR defines personal data broadly to include any information that can directly or indirectly identify an individual, from names and email addresses to location data and IP addresses. This protection extends to data collected in both online and offline settings, ensuring that privacy is maintained across all platforms.

2. **Empowerment of Individuals**: GDPR grants several specific rights to individuals, including the rights to access, correct, and delete their data (often called the "Right to Be Forgotten"). This empowerment aims to create a balanced relationship between individuals and the companies that hold their data, putting more control back into the hands of the individual.
3. **Promoting Responsible Data Management**: Companies are required to integrate data privacy into their systems by default, following principles of "privacy by design." They must only collect the data they need, store it for as long as necessary, and secure it against breaches. This proactive approach helps organizations avoid privacy issues before they arise and promotes a culture of responsible data management.

1.4 The Impact of GDPR on Non-EU Countries

A unique aspect of GDPR is its extraterritorial scope. The regulation applies not only to EU-based companies but also to any organization worldwide that offers goods or services to, or monitors the behavior of, EU residents. This means that companies in the United States, Canada, and beyond must comply with GDPR if they handle data from EU residents.

This extraterritoriality has created ripple effects worldwide. Many companies have updated their data practices to align with GDPR, even if they do not have a physical presence in the EU, as a way to ensure compliance. As a result, GDPR has influenced the development of data privacy laws globally, with countries like Brazil, Japan, and South Korea creating their own GDPR-inspired regulations.

1.5 Benefits of GDPR for Individuals and Organizations

While GDPR places significant compliance obligations on organizations, it also benefits both individuals and businesses by fostering a more transparent, trustworthy environment for data use.

For Individuals: GDPR provides individuals with clear rights and protections regarding their data. They have more control, can access and manage their information, and are assured that organizations must keep their data safe. These rights provide individuals with a greater sense of trust and security in their interactions with companies.

For Organizations: Although the path to compliance can be complex, GDPR offers long-term benefits for businesses. Companies that comply with GDPR can build greater trust with their customers, reducing reputational risk. By embedding privacy into their operations, businesses can differentiate themselves as responsible data stewards and potentially avoid costly breaches and penalties.

1.6 Summary: GDPR in Today's Digital World

In today's data-driven world, GDPR serves as a necessary framework to protect individuals from the risks associated with widespread data collection. By prioritizing transparency, accountability, and individual rights, GDPR aims to create a digital landscape where privacy is respected, and data is protected. For U.S. audiences, understanding GDPR means understanding how data rights are evolving globally and why data protection is becoming a central concern for governments, companies, and individuals alike.

Chapter 2:
Scope of GDPR

Chapter 2.1: Scope of GDPR

The General Data Protection Regulation (GDPR) has a broad scope, affecting both EU-based and non-EU businesses. Any company operating within the European Union must comply, regardless of whether its customers or employees are EU citizens. Additionally, businesses outside the EU, including those in the U.S., must follow GDPR rules if they offer goods or services to EU residents—even for free—or monitor the online behavior of individuals in the EU. This means that a U.S. e-commerce store selling products to French customers, or a travel website using cookies to track German visitors' browsing habits, must comply with GDPR regulations. This broad territorial scope makes GDPR a global standard in data privacy.

Beyond where the law applies, GDPR also defines what types of data fall under its protection. The regulation covers any information that can identify a person, such as names, emails, IP addresses, and even behavioral data collected through tracking technologies. It applies to both digital and paper records, whether stored in databases or spreadsheets. However, GDPR does not apply to personal, household activities, such as maintaining a contact list for personal use.

For U.S. citizens, GDPR can have several direct and indirect effects. If an American lives, works, or travels in the EU, their personal data is protected under GDPR, granting them rights such as accessing their data, correcting inaccuracies, and requesting the deletion of their information under the "right to be forgotten." Additionally, many U.S. companies that interact with EU residents have adopted GDPR-like policies, improving data transparency, giving users more control over their personal information, and strengthening security measures. This benefits all users, including Americans, by reducing risks like identity theft and unauthorized data sharing.

However, GDPR also introduces changes that may affect digital services for U.S. users. Americans using global platforms may notice more frequent consent pop-ups when websites request permission to collect their data. Some businesses, particularly smaller ones, may even choose to stop offering services to EU customers to avoid the complexity of compliance, potentially limiting access to certain products or platforms. Overall, GDPR's reach extends far beyond Europe, influencing data protection standards worldwide and shaping how businesses handle personal information.

The scope of GDPR is extensive, with significant implications even for U.S. citizens and businesses.

The General Data Protection Regulation (GDPR) extends its reach beyond the European Union (EU) through its extraterritorial provisions, impacting organizations worldwide that handle the personal data of individuals within the EU. This means that even if a company is not physically located within the EU, it must comply with the GDPR if it engages in certain activities involving EU residents' data.

The General Data Protection Regulation (GDPR) applies not only to businesses within the European Union but also to non-EU organizations in specific situations. One key scenario is when a company offers goods or services to individuals residing in the EU. For example, if a U.S.-based e-commerce business sells products online and allows European customers to make purchases, the GDPR applies to that company, even if it has no physical presence in the EU. This is true regardless of whether the company charges for its services. Certain factors indicate an intention to serve EU customers, such as displaying prices in euros, providing website content in European languages like German or French, or using country-specific domain names such as ".de" for Germany or ".fr" for France. Additionally, running marketing campaigns that specifically mention EU customers or target EU audiences can also bring a company under GDPR's jurisdiction.

Another major scenario where GDPR applies to non-EU businesses is when they monitor the behavior of EU residents. For instance, if a U.S. social media company or an online retailer uses cookies, tracking pixels, or other technologies to collect data on European visitors to analyze their preferences or predict purchasing behavior, they must comply with GDPR. This includes profiling activities, such as creating personalized recommendations based on browsing history, tracking user interactions, or using AI-driven tools to predict consumer interests. Even if a company does not directly sell products to the EU, merely collecting and analyzing data from European users for marketing or research purposes is enough to trigger GDPR compliance requirements. Essentially, any business that actively engages with or tracks EU individuals must ensure that it follows GDPR guidelines, including obtaining proper consent and protecting users' personal data.

Non-EU businesses that fall within the scope of the General Data Protection Regulation (GDPR) must comply with its stringent data protection requirements. This includes adhering to core data protection principles, ensuring that personal data is processed lawfully, transparently, and for a specific purpose. Additionally, organizations must respect the rights of data subjects, such as granting individuals access to their data, allowing corrections, enabling data deletion upon request, and providing data portability options. To safeguard personal information, companies are required to implement appropriate technical and organizational security measures to prevent unauthorized access, breaches, or misuse of data.

Furthermore, non-EU businesses that are subject to GDPR may be required to appoint an EU-based representative to act as a point of contact for both data subjects and regulatory authorities. The enforcement of GDPR is rigorous, with significant penalties for non-compliance. For example, in August 2024, Uber was fined €290 million by the Dutch Data Protection Authority for improperly transferring driver data from the EU to the U.S., underscoring the regulation's reach beyond Europe. This case serves as a stark reminder that GDPR applies to businesses worldwide if they process EU residents' data. The regulation's extraterritorial scope ensures that European individuals' data is protected, regardless of where the company handling it is based, reinforcing GDPR as a global standard for data privacy and security.

Indirect Impacts on U.S. Citizens

The General Data Protection Regulation (GDPR) has had a significant indirect impact on U.S. citizens, shaping privacy laws, influencing business practices, and increasing awareness of data protection. One of the most notable effects is its role in inspiring U.S. state-level privacy laws, such as the California Consumer Privacy Act (CCPA). Similar to GDPR, the CCPA grants Californians rights like accessing personal data, requesting its deletion, and opting out of data sales. As concerns over digital privacy grow, more states—or even the federal government—may introduce stricter regulations to protect consumer data, following GDPR's lead.

Beyond legislation, GDPR has pushed companies worldwide to adopt stronger privacy standards.

Many businesses, especially those with international customers, have chosen to apply GDPR-compliant policies across all markets to simplify compliance and build customer trust. For instance, major tech companies like Apple and Microsoft have extended privacy protections globally, giving U.S. users more control over their data, even when not legally required. Additionally, international agreements like the EU-U.S. Data Privacy Framework ensure that when personal data is transferred between the EU and the U.S., it is handled with the same level of care required under GDPR, further enhancing privacy protections.

Perhaps one of the most widespread impacts of GDPR is the heightened awareness of personal data rights. The regulation has sparked global conversations about data privacy, making U.S. citizens more conscious of how their information is collected, shared, and used. As a result, consumers are increasingly seeking out companies that prioritize data security and transparency. For example, more users are choosing privacy-focused search engines like DuckDuckGo over traditional options or using browser extensions that block tracking. Overall, while GDPR was designed to protect EU residents, its influence has led to stronger privacy protections, better business practices, and a more privacy-aware society in the U.S. and beyond.

Challenges and Opportunities for U.S. Citizens

The implementation of GDPR presents both challenges and opportunities for U.S. citizens, even though the regulation primarily applies to EU residents. One of the most significant benefits is greater transparency, as businesses are now required to clearly disclose how they collect, use, and store personal data. This empowers users by giving them more control and awareness over their information, leading to better decision-making when engaging with digital services. However, GDPR also introduces certain inconveniences, such as frequent consent pop-ups on websites asking for permission to track user data. While these measures enhance privacy, they can sometimes feel intrusive or disrupt the user experience. Additionally, some companies, especially smaller businesses, may limit their services in certain regions to avoid the complexities of GDPR compliance, potentially restricting access to digital platforms or products for some users. On the positive side, GDPR has helped increase consumer trust, as companies that align with its principles are generally perceived as more responsible and secure. This has led many businesses, even outside the EU, to adopt similar privacy policies to build credibility and protect their customers. In the long run, these changes contribute to a safer and more privacy-conscious online environment for everyone.

How Does This Affect Habits?

GDPR has influenced online habits by encouraging users to be more mindful of their privacy settings, cookie preferences, and the platforms they engage with. Many people now spend more time managing their data permissions, particularly on websites that ship to the EU or services that collect personal information, such as fitness trackers, travel apps, or social media platforms. This regulation has also raised awareness about digital privacy, making individuals more cautious about how their personal information is collected and used.

At its core, GDPR ensures that any data capable of identifying an individual—whether directly, like a name or address, or indirectly, through behaviors such as shopping habits or social media interactions—is protected. Organizations that collect, store, or process such data must follow strict guidelines to handle it responsibly and transparently. This protection applies to a wide range of personal information, from basic identifiers to more sensitive details, such as health records or online activity. By setting these standards, GDPR has reshaped the way businesses approach data privacy and how users interact with digital services.

Key Categories of Protected Data: How is Personal and Non-Personal Data handled under GDPR

GDPR protects a wide range of personal data, ensuring that individuals have control over how their information is collected, stored, and used. This includes basic identity details such as names, addresses (including email), and phone numbers. Additionally, web and device data, such as IP addresses, cookies, browsing history, and location tracking, also fall under GDPR protection, as they can be used to identify individuals or track their online behavior.

Certain types of personal data receive even stricter protection under GDPR. Sensitive categories include racial or ethnic origin, political opinions, religious or philosophical beliefs, trade union membership, genetic and biometric data (such as fingerprints or facial recognition), health information, and details related to sexual orientation or behavior. Financial data, including bank account numbers, credit card details, and transactional records, are also safeguarded, as are professional and educational records, such as employment history, job roles, academic qualifications, and certifications. Other unique identifiers, including Social Security numbers, passport numbers, and license plate numbers, also fall within GDPR's protection.

Health data is a particularly sensitive category under GDPR, encompassing any information related to a person's physical or mental health. This includes medical conditions, test results, health history, and records of past, present, or future medical treatments. Healthcare services data, such as prescriptions, doctor's notes, and surgical records, are also covered. Additionally, genetic and biometric data—like DNA test results, fingerprints, and facial recognition used for health purposes—are subject to strict regulations. Even lifestyle and well-being data collected by health and fitness apps, such as heart rate, sleep patterns, and exercise routines, fall under GDPR when they can be linked to an individual.

However, GDPR does not apply to anonymized data, as long as it is processed in a way that ensures it cannot be traced back to a specific person. This distinction is crucial for businesses and researchers handling large datasets, as proper anonymization techniques allow data to be used without violating privacy laws. By setting these strict standards, GDPR aims to create a more secure and transparent environment for handling personal information, ensuring that individuals' data is protected no matter how it is collected or processed.

Key GDPR Requirements for Processing Health Data

Because health data is classified as a special category under GDPR, its processing is generally restricted unless specific conditions are met. One of the primary requirements is explicit consent, meaning individuals must clearly agree to their health data being collected and used. However, there are exceptions where processing is permitted without consent, such as when it is necessary to comply with legal obligations or serve the public interest, including safeguarding public health or ensuring workplace safety. Additionally, health data may be processed for medical purposes, such as preventive care, diagnosis, or treatment. Scientific research and statistical analysis are also allowed under GDPR, provided that organizations implement privacy safeguards, such as pseudonymization, which ensures data is not directly linked to individuals.

Organizations handling health data must follow strict protection measures to comply with GDPR. This includes data minimization, meaning only the necessary information should be collected, along with the use of encryption and other security measures to prevent breaches. Regular audits and risk assessments are required to ensure compliance, and individuals must have rights over their data, including the ability to access, correct, or delete it. These rules apply to a wide range of organizations, including hospitals, clinics, health insurers, pharmaceutical companies conducting research, and developers of health apps and wearable technology.

Ultimately, GDPR ensures that health data is handled with care, balancing individual privacy with the need for essential medical, legal, and research-based processing. While GDPR is designed to protect EU residents, its influence extends beyond Europe, indirectly benefiting U.S. citizens by encouraging stronger global privacy practices. As businesses worldwide adopt GDPR-style protections, individuals gain better control over their personal data, enhanced security, and greater transparency in how their information is handled. This shift toward prioritizing privacy may also inspire future improvements in U.S. privacy laws, setting a new standard for data protection worldwide.

Chapter 2.2: Impact on Businesses

Chapter 2.2: The General Data Protection Regulation (GDPR) has significantly impacted businesses, particularly those that handle the personal data of individuals in the European Union (EU). To comply with GDPR, businesses must follow strict guidelines on data collection, processing, and storage. This includes obtaining **explicit consent** from individuals before collecting their data and providing clear explanations about how their information will be used. Additionally, companies must ensure that individuals can exercise their **data subject rights**, such as accessing, correcting, deleting, or restricting the processing of their data. Businesses need efficient processes to respond to these requests in a timely manner.

Many organizations, especially those that process large amounts of personal data, are required to appoint a **Data Protection Officer (DPO)** to oversee GDPR compliance and data protection strategies. Failure to comply with GDPR can lead to **severe financial penalties**, with fines reaching up to €20 million or 4% of a company's global annual revenue, whichever is higher. Additionally, businesses must be prepared for **data breach notifications**, as GDPR requires certain breaches to be reported to supervisory authorities within **72 hours**. If a breach poses a high risk to individuals' rights, affected users must also be informed.

GDPR has also reshaped **marketing and sales practices**, particularly in digital marketing and customer communication. Companies must now obtain **explicit consent** before sending promotional emails or collecting customer data for targeted advertising. They must also offer easy opt-out options to respect consumer privacy preferences. While these regulations impose new challenges, compliance with GDPR can ultimately enhance a company's **reputation and customer trust** by demonstrating a strong commitment to data privacy and protection. Conversely, failing to meet GDPR standards can damage a business's reputation and lead to legal consequences.

Overall, GDPR aims to provide individuals with greater control over their personal data while ensuring businesses handle information **responsibly and transparently**. Though the regulation introduces strict requirements, it also encourages better data management practices, helping businesses build stronger relationships with customers in an era where privacy and security are more important than ever.

Relevance of GDPR in USA

The General Data Protection Regulation (GDPR) is highly relevant to U.S. businesses, as its **extraterritorial scope** applies to any company that processes the personal data of individuals in the EU. This means that if a U.S. business offers goods or services to EU residents or tracks their online behavior—such as through cookies, analytics, or targeted advertising—it must comply with GDPR regulations. Additionally, U.S. companies must respect **data subject rights**, ensuring that EU customers can access, correct, delete, or restrict the processing of their personal data upon request.

Another key area of impact is **data transfers** between the EU and the U.S. Businesses must implement strong protection measures when handling EU personal data, such as using **Standard Contractual Clauses (SCCs)** or other approved mechanisms to ensure compliance. Failure to meet GDPR requirements can lead to **severe penalties**, with fines reaching up to **€20 million or 4% of global annual revenue**, making non-compliance both a financial and reputational risk for U.S. companies.

Beyond legal obligations, GDPR has set a **global standard for data privacy**, influencing regulations in the U.S., such as the **California Consumer Privacy Act (CCPA)**, which grants similar rights to California residents. As more states consider stricter privacy laws, GDPR continues to shape the broader conversation around data protection in the U.S. In essence, GDPR affects any American business that interacts with EU residents' data, encouraging stronger privacy practices and compliance measures across industries.

Who Does GDPR Apply To in the U.S.?

Let's break down who and what GDPR applies to—whether you're a consumer, worker, healthcare professional, or business owner in the U.S.

1. **Businesses in the U.S. Handling EU Data**

Does your U.S. business deal with customers, employees, or clients in the EU?

If you run a business in the U.S. and you interact with EU residents—whether by selling products, offering services, or processing personal information—GDPR applies to you. So, even if your business is based in the U.S., you must follow these rules if you handle data from the EU.

Everyday Example

You run an online store in the U.S. that ships products to customers in the EU. You collect personal information from these customers, like their names, shipping addresses, and payment details. According to GDPR, you must:

- Get clear consent before collecting or using their personal data.
- Make sure their data is secure and only kept for as long as necessary.
- Allow them to access their data and delete it if they ask.

Checklist for U.S. Businesses

Does your business need to follow GDPR?

- **Do you sell to EU customers or clients?**
- **Do you track data on EU users (like website activity)?**
- **Do you process sensitive data (like health info or payment details) from EU residents?**

If you answered "yes," then you need to comply with GDPR.

2. Healthcare Providers in the U.S. with EU Patients

Do you treat patients from the EU or handle their personal health data?

If you're a healthcare provider in the U.S. and you offer services to people in the EU—whether through telemedicine, online consultations, or any other remote service—GDPR applies to the personal health data of these patients.

Everyday Example

You're a U.S. doctor who offers telehealth consultations to patients in the EU. You collect and store sensitive health data (like medical history and treatment plans). Under GDPR, you need to:

- Ensure that the patient's data is securely stored and protected.
- Ask for explicit consent before collecting sensitive health information.
- Provide patients the right to see or delete their health data.

Checklist for U.S. Healthcare Providers

Does GDPR affect your healthcare practice?

- **Do you treat or consult with patients from the EU?**
- **Do you store health data for EU residents?**
- **Do you share or transfer health data across borders?**

If you answered "yes," you'll need to comply with GDPR to protect the personal health data of your EU patients.

3. U.S. Consumers Who Use EU-Based Services

Even if you're not running a business or providing healthcare services, GDPR can still affect you as a

consumer. If you use websites, apps, or online services from companies that also operate in the EU, these companies need to follow GDPR when handling your personal information.

Everyday Example

You sign up for an app that tracks your health and fitness, or maybe you use a website to buy products from Europe. These services may collect data about your activity, preferences, or location. Under GDPR:

- They must get your permission to collect your data.
- They must explain how your data will be used and protected.
- You have the right to request that your data be deleted at any time.

Checklist for U.S. Consumers

While the General Data Protection Regulation (GDPR) is a European Union law, it indirectly impacts online experiences in the United States in several ways:

1. Website Practices

Many global websites and services, even those accessible in the U.S., have adjusted their privacy policies and implemented GDPR-compliant features. For example:

- **Cookie Consent Banners**: You may see pop-ups asking for consent to track your activity using cookies.

- **Privacy Policy Updates**: Sites often clarify how they collect and process personal data, even for non-EU users.

2. Access to Services

Some websites or services block U.S. users entirely to avoid compliance complexities. You might encounter messages like "This service is unavailable in your location."

3. Data Privacy Awareness

GDPR has encouraged broader awareness of data privacy globally. Many U.S. users have become more conscious of:

- Opting out of data collection.
- Reviewing terms of service.
- Managing permissions for apps and services.

4. Impact on U.S. Data Laws

GDPR has inspired U.S. states, like California, to adopt similar regulations (e.g., the California Consumer Privacy Act, CCPA). These laws give U.S. users some rights to control their data, mirroring GDPR principles.

Does GDPR Apply to Small Businesses in the U.S.?

Yes! GDPR applies to **small businesses** too—whether you have 5 employees or 500. If your business deals with EU data in any way, you need to follow GDPR rules.

Yes, **GDPR can apply to small businesses in the U.S.** if they meet certain conditions, even though it is a European Union regulation. The law governs how businesses process the personal data of individuals located in the EU, regardless of where the business itself is based.

When Does GDPR Apply to U.S. Small Businesses?

U.S.-based small businesses must comply with GDPR if they:

1. **Offer Goods or Services to EU Residents**
    - Actively market products or services to people in the EU.
    - Accept payments in EU currencies or offer shipping to EU countries.
2. **Monitor Behavior of EU Residents**
    - Track or analyze the online behavior of EU individuals (e.g., through cookies, analytics, or profiling).
    - Operate websites that collect data on EU residents (e.g., IP addresses, browsing history).
3. **Process EU Personal Data**
    - Handle any personal data of EU individuals as part of business operations, even indirectly.

Everyday Example

Let's say you run a small online boutique in the U.S. that ships to Europe. You collect customer data (like names, addresses, and payment details) from people in the EU. Under GDPR:

- You need to have a clear privacy policy explaining how you use customer data.
- You must ask customers for permission before collecting sensitive data.
- You must keep the data secure and provide customers with the option to delete it.

Examples of U.S. Small Businesses Affected by GDPR

- **E-commerce sites** shipping to the EU.
- **Freelancers or consultants** working with EU clients.
- **Software as a Service (SaaS) companies** with EU users.
- **Travel and hospitality businesses** booking services for EU residents.

Key Requirements for U.S. Small Businesses

If GDPR applies, small businesses must:

1. Obtain **explicit consent** from EU residents before collecting personal data.
2. Maintain a clear and transparent **privacy policy**.
3. Allow individuals to exercise their rights (e.g., access, rectification, deletion of data).
4. Implement strong **data protection measures** like encryption and secure storage.

5. Notify EU authorities and affected individuals in case of a **data breach**.

Penalties for Non-Compliance

Non-compliance with GDPR can result in significant fines, even for small businesses. Penalties can be as high as €20 million or 4% of annual global turnover, whichever is higher.

Best Practices for U.S. Small Businesses

- Assess whether GDPR applies to your operations.
- Consult with legal experts to ensure compliance.
- Use GDPR-compliant tools for data storage, processing, and communication.
- Regularly review and update data privacy practices.

Key Takeaway

Even small businesses in the U.S. may fall under GDPR if they handle the personal data of EU residents. Proactively addressing compliance can mitigate risks and build trust with customers globally.

Checklist for Small Businesses

Does GDPR apply to your small business?

- **Do you collect personal data from EU customers or clients?**
- **Do you use online tools that track personal information?**

- **Do you handle sensitive data, like health or financial information?**

If you answered "yes," even a small business must follow GDPR.

Chapter 3:
Information Protected Under GDPR

The General Data Protection Regulation (GDPR) protects a wide range of personal data to ensure the privacy and security of individuals within the European Union. Here are the key types of information covered under GDPR:

Basic Identity Information

- Name: Any individual's full name.
- Address: Residential or mailing address.
- Identification Numbers: National ID numbers, passport numbers, and other unique identifiers.

Contact Information

- Phone Numbers: Mobile, landline, and work phone numbers.
- Email Addresses: Personal and professional email addresses.

Web Data

- IP Addresses: Internet Protocol addresses used to identify devices online.
- Cookie Data: Information stored in cookies that track online behavior.

- RFID Tags: Data from Radio Frequency Identification tags used in various applications.

Biometric Data

- Fingerprint Scans: Used for identification and security purposes.
- Retina Scans: Biometric data used for secure access and identification.

Health and Genetic Data

- Medical History: Information about past and current medical conditions.
- Genetic Information: Data related to genetic tests and hereditary conditions.

Special Categories of Data

- Racial or Ethnic Origin: Information about an individual's race or ethnicity.
- Political Opinions: Data regarding political beliefs and affiliations.
- Religious or Philosophical Beliefs: Information about religious practices or philosophical views.
- Trade-Union Membership: Data about membership in trade unions.
- Sexual Orientation: Information about an individual's sexual preferences and orientation.

Financial Information

- Bank Account Details: Information related to bank accounts and transactions.
- Credit Card Information: Data used for payment processing and financial transactions.

Location Data

- GPS Data: Information from GPS devices that track location.
- Location Data from Mobile Devices: Data collected from smartphones and other mobile devices.

Behavioral Data

- Browsing History: Information about websites visited and online activities.
- Purchase History: Data related to past purchases and shopping behavior.

GDPR ensures that organizations handling these types of personal data must adhere to strict guidelines for data protection, including obtaining explicit consent, providing transparency about data usage, and implementing robust security measures. This comprehensive approach aims to safeguard individuals' privacy and enhance trust in how their personal information is managed

Consent

Under GDPR, obtaining valid consent for data processing involves several key steps to ensure that it is freely given, specific, informed, and unambiguous. Here's a detailed look at how consent is obtained:

Freely Given

- **Voluntary Basis**: Consent must be given on a voluntary basis, meaning individuals should have a genuine choice and control over whether to consent. It should not be coerced or conditional on the provision of a service unless necessary for that service.

Specific

- **Purpose Limitation**: Consent must be specific to the purpose for which the data is being collected. If data is to be used for multiple purposes, consent must be obtained for each purpose separately. For example, if a company wants to use an email address for both marketing and account verification, it must obtain consent for both uses.

Informed

- **Clear Information**: Individuals must be provided with clear and comprehensive information about the data processing activities. This includes details about what data will be collected, how it will be used, who it will be shared with, and the rights of the data subject. This information should be presented in an easily understandable format, avoiding legal jargon.

Unambiguous

- **Affirmative Action**: Consent must be given through a clear affirmative action, such as ticking a box on a website, selecting technical settings, or another statement or conduct that clearly indicates agreement. Pre-ticked boxes or implied consent are not acceptable under GDPR.

Documentation and Management

- **Record Keeping**: Organizations must keep records of consent to demonstrate compliance. This includes details of when, how, and what information was provided to the individual at the time of consent.
- **Withdrawal of Consent**: Individuals must be informed of their right to withdraw consent at any time, and it should be as easy to withdraw consent as it is to give it.

Practical Examples

- **Online Forms**: When signing up for a newsletter, users might be presented with a checkbox to consent to receiving emails. The checkbox should not be pre-ticked, and the form should include a link to the privacy policy explaining how their data will be used.
- **Mobile Apps**: When installing a mobile app, users might be asked to consent to data collection for personalized ads. The app should

provide clear information about what data will be collected and how it will be used, with an option to opt-out.

By following these principles, organizations can ensure that they obtain valid consent in compliance with GDPR, thereby protecting individuals' privacy rights and fostering trust.

Chapter 4:
How GDPR Shows Up in Daily Life- Real Life Scenarios

GDPR impacts various everyday activities, even for U.S. residents, when businesses handle data from EU customers. For example, if you order a gift from an online store in the U.S. that also ships to Europe, the company must comply with GDPR regulations. This means they must ask for permission before using your personal data—such as your name, shipping address, and payment details—and provide a clear privacy policy outlining how your information is used.

Similarly, if you use telemedicine healthcare services to consult with a doctor based in Europe, any personal health data you share must be securely handled under GDPR. This includes your medical history, prescriptions, or test results. The doctor or service provider must also allow you to access, correct, or request deletion of your data if you choose.

Even using a fitness app that serves EU customers can bring GDPR protections into play. If the app tracks your daily steps, calorie intake, or workout routines, it must clearly explain how your data is used, protect your personal information, and provide an option to delete your data if you no longer want it stored. These requirements ensure that businesses handling personal data remain transparent, secure, and accountable, benefiting users worldwide, even outside the EU.

In addition to these scenarios, consider using social media platforms that have a global user base, including many from the EU. These platforms must adhere to GDPR when processing data from EU users, which means they must provide clear consent mechanisms, data access rights, and robust security measures. This can indirectly benefit U.S. users by promoting higher standards of data protection and transparency.

Moreover, if you subscribe to a newsletter from a European company, GDPR requires that the company obtain explicit consent before sending you emails and provide an easy way to unsubscribe. This ensures that your inbox is not flooded with unwanted communications and that your preferences are respected.

Overall, GDPR's influence extends beyond the EU, promoting better data practices and enhancing privacy protections for users globally. This regulatory framework encourages businesses to adopt more transparent, secure, and user-centric approaches to data management, ultimately fostering greater trust and accountability in the digital ecosystem.

Here are some additional real-life examples of GDPR in action:

Online Retailers

When you shop online from a retailer that serves EU customers, GDPR requires the retailer to obtain your explicit consent before collecting and processing your personal data. This includes your name, address, payment information, and browsing behavior. The retailer must also provide a clear privacy policy explaining how your data will be used and offer options to access, correct, or delete your data.

Social Media Platforms

Social media platforms like Facebook and Twitter must comply with GDPR when handling data from EU users. This means they need to provide clear consent mechanisms for data collection, allow users to access and delete their data, and ensure robust security measures to protect personal information. For example, Facebook implemented a feature that allows users to download a copy of their data and see how it is being used.

Healthcare Services

Healthcare providers, including telemedicine services, must adhere to GDPR when dealing with EU patients' data. This includes ensuring the secure handling of sensitive health information, such as medical history and test results. Patients must be informed about how their data is used and have the right to access, correct, or delete their information.

Financial Institutions

Banks and financial institutions that serve EU customers must comply with GDPR by implementing strict data protection measures. This includes obtaining consent for data processing, providing transparency about data usage, and ensuring the security of financial information. For instance, a bank must inform customers about how their transaction data is used and offer options to manage their privacy settings.

Mobile Apps

Mobile apps that collect data from EU users, such as fitness trackers or weather apps, must comply with GDPR. This involves obtaining user consent for data collection, providing clear information about data usage, and allowing users to delete their data. For example, a fitness app must explain how it uses data like steps taken and calories burned, and offer an option to delete this data if the user chooses.

Educational Institutions

Universities and schools that handle data from EU students must comply with GDPR. This includes protecting personal information such as student records, grades, and contact details. Educational institutions must inform students about how their data is used and provide options to access and correct their information.

These examples illustrate how GDPR influences various sectors and ensures that businesses handling personal data remain transparent, secure, and accountable, benefiting users worldwide.

Summary

In summary the General Data Protection Regulation (GDPR) has a broad impact, even for Americans, affecting businesses, healthcare providers, and consumers. **U.S. businesses** that interact with EU customers, clients, or employees must comply with GDPR regulations, ensuring that personal data is collected, stored, and processed responsibly. **Healthcare providers** offering services to EU patients must implement strict data protection measures, safeguarding sensitive health information and granting patients control over their records. **Consumers** using apps or services with EU customers should be aware of how their data is collected, shared, and protected under GDPR. Whether shopping online, using telemedicine, or tracking fitness data, GDPR influences privacy practices across industries, encouraging greater transparency and security worldwide.

In the next chapter, we'll dive into the practical steps of GDPR compliance, including how businesses and individuals can make sure they're following the law and protecting personal data. Stay with us as we explore how GDPR impacts you, step by step!

Part 2: Implications of GDPR in the United States

Implications of GDPR for the United States

The General Data Protection Regulation (GDPR) has significant implications for businesses and organizations in the United States, even though it is an EU regulation. Its extraterritorial scope affects any U.S. entity that processes personal data of individuals in the EU. Below are the key implications:

1. Extraterritorial Applicability

The General Data Protection Regulation (GDPR) extends its jurisdiction beyond the European Union (EU), impacting non-EU businesses under specific conditions. Notably, the GDPR applies to organizations outside the EU if they offer goods or services to individuals within the EU, irrespective of whether payment is involved. This means that even free services targeted at EU residents can subject a non-EU company to GDPR compliance requirements. Additionally, the regulation encompasses businesses that monitor the behavior of individuals within the EU, such as using cookies or analytics to track online activities. Consequently, U.S.-based companies with customers or users in the EU are obligated to adhere to GDPR provisions, regardless of the company's physical location. This extraterritorial applicability ensures that the data rights of EU residents are protected globally, compelling international organizations to align their data processing practices with GDPR standards. Non-compliance can result in substantial fines, reaching up to €20 million or 4% of the company's annual global turnover, whichever is higher. Therefore, it is imperative for U.S. companies engaging with EU residents to thoroughly assess their data handling practices and implement necessary measures to achieve GDPR compliance.

2. Data Subject Rights

The General Data Protection Regulation (GDPR) endows individuals within the European Union (EU) with specific rights over their personal data, which organizations—including U.S.-based companies—must uphold when processing such information.

One fundamental right is the **Right to Access**, allowing individuals to obtain confirmation about whether their personal data is being processed and, if so, access to that data along with information about the processing activities. This ensures transparency and enables individuals to verify the lawfulness of the processing.

Another pivotal right is the **Right to Erasure**, commonly known as the "Right to be Forgotten." This permits individuals to request the deletion of their personal data under certain circumstances, such as when the data is no longer necessary for the purposes it was collected, or if the individual withdraws consent upon which the processing is based. This right empowers individuals to have their data removed, enhancing control over personal information.

The **Right to Data Portability** allows individuals to receive their personal data in a structured, commonly used, and machine-readable format, and to transmit that data to another controller without hindrance. This facilitates the free flow of personal data across service providers, promoting competition and user autonomy.

Additionally, the **Right to Object** enables individuals to object to the processing of their personal data, particularly when processing is based on legitimate interests or for direct marketing purposes. Upon objection, the processing must cease unless the controller demonstrates compelling legitimate grounds that override the interests, rights, and freedoms of the individual.

For U.S. organizations processing EU residents' data, compliance with these rights necessitates the development and implementation of robust systems and processes. This includes establishing clear procedures for handling data subject requests, ensuring timely responses within the GDPR-mandated timeframes, and maintaining accurate records of processing activities. Organizations must also provide easily accessible channels for individuals to exercise their rights and ensure that staff are trained to recognize and appropriately handle such requests. Failure to comply can result in significant penalties, emphasizing the importance of integrating these requirements into the organization's data governance framework.

3. Data Protection Obligations

The General Data Protection Regulation (GDPR) imposes stringent data protection obligations on businesses, including U.S. companies that process the personal data of individuals within the European Union. Compliance with these requirements necessitates a structured approach to data handling, ensuring that organizations implement safeguards that align with GDPR principles. One fundamental requirement is **data minimization**, which mandates that businesses collect only the personal data strictly necessary for a specific, legitimate purpose. This principle prevents excessive data collection and reduces the risk of unnecessary data exposure. Organizations must define clear objectives for data processing and avoid retaining personal information longer than needed.

Another critical obligation is **accountability and documentation**, requiring businesses to maintain detailed records of their processing activities. This includes documenting what personal data is collected, the purpose of processing, data retention policies, and any third parties with whom data is shared. Organizations must also designate a Data Protection Officer (DPO) when required and conduct Data Protection Impact Assessments (DPIAs) for high-risk processing activities. Proper documentation not only demonstrates compliance but also ensures businesses can respond effectively to regulatory inquiries.

To safeguard personal data, businesses must implement **robust security measures** to protect against breaches and unauthorized access. GDPR encourages encryption, anonymization, and pseudonymization as techniques to enhance data security. Businesses must also conduct regular security assessments, establish incident response plans, and ensure that employees handling personal data are trained in security best practices. In the event of a data breach, companies must notify the relevant supervisory authority within 72 hours (about 6 days) and inform affected individuals if the breach poses a significant risk to their rights and freedoms.

Failure to comply with these obligations can result in severe financial penalties, even for companies operating outside the EU. GDPR enforcement allows for fines of up to €20 million or 4% of a company's global annual turnover, whichever is higher. Beyond financial penalties, non-compliance can damage an organization's reputation, erode consumer trust, and create legal vulnerabilities. As data protection regulations evolve worldwide, adhering to GDPR's stringent requirements can position businesses ahead of emerging privacy laws, ensuring long-term compliance and data security.

4. Privacy Notices and Consent

To comply with the General Data Protection Regulation (GDPR), U.S. companies that process the personal data of EU residents must revise their privacy policies to ensure full transparency and adherence to legal requirements. Organizations are required to provide clear and comprehensive privacy notices that explicitly state how personal data is collected, used, stored, and shared. These notices must be written in simple, easily understandable language, avoiding legal jargon to ensure that individuals fully comprehend how their information is being handled. Companies must specify the categories of data collected, the purpose of processing, the legal basis for such processing, data retention periods, and whether data is shared with third parties or transferred outside the EU.

Another crucial requirement under GDPR is obtaining explicit consent from individuals before collecting and processing their personal data, particularly in cases where no other legal basis applies. Consent must be freely given, specific, informed, and unambiguous, which means companies cannot use pre-checked boxes or assume consent through inactivity. Instead, users must actively agree to data collection, typically through clear opt-in mechanisms. Furthermore, companies must document and store records of consent to demonstrate compliance in case of regulatory scrutiny.

In addition to obtaining consent, businesses must also provide users with the ability to withdraw their consent easily at any time. GDPR mandates that withdrawing consent should be as straightforward as giving it, requiring organizations to implement accessible mechanisms, such as a simple opt-out option or preference settings within user accounts. Companies must ensure that once consent is withdrawn, data processing ceases immediately unless another legal basis applies. Failure to comply with these transparency and consent requirements can lead to severe penalties, including fines of up to €20 million or 4% of a company's global revenue. Beyond financial repercussions, inadequate privacy policies can erode consumer trust, making GDPR compliance not only a legal necessity but also a vital component of responsible data governance and corporate integrity.

5. Data Breach Notification

Under the General Data Protection Regulation (GDPR), businesses that experience a data breach must adhere to strict notification requirements to ensure transparency and mitigate potential harm. Organizations are required to report any personal data breach to the relevant supervisory authority within 72 hours of becoming aware of the incident, unless the breach is unlikely to result in a risk to individuals' rights and freedoms. The notification must include a detailed description of the nature of the breach, the types of personal data affected, the approximate number of impacted individuals, and the potential consequences. Additionally, organizations must outline the corrective actions taken to address the breach and prevent future occurrences.

In cases where the data breach is likely to result in a high risk to the rights and freedoms of individuals, businesses must also inform the affected individuals without undue delay. This ensures that those impacted are aware of the potential risks and can take necessary precautions, such as updating passwords, monitoring financial transactions, or being vigilant against identity theft. The notification to individuals must be clear and concise, explaining the nature of the breach, its likely consequences, and any recommended steps to mitigate risks.

Failure to comply with GDPR's breach notification requirements can result in severe penalties. Regulatory authorities can impose fines of up to €10 million or 2% of a company's global annual turnover, whichever is higher, for failing to notify the relevant authority within the prescribed timeframe. If an organization fails to inform affected individuals in cases where high risks are involved, fines can be even higher. Beyond financial penalties, a mishandled breach can severely damage a company's reputation, leading to a loss of customer trust and potential legal action. Therefore, organizations must establish robust breach detection, response, and reporting mechanisms to ensure compliance with GDPR and safeguard individuals' personal data.

6. Appointment of Data Protection Officers (DPOs)

U.S. businesses may be required to appoint a **Data Protection Officer (DPO)** if they process **large amounts of sensitive data**, such as health records or biometric information, or if they engage in **large-scale monitoring of EU individuals**, including tracking online behavior through analytics or targeted advertising. The DPO is responsible for ensuring GDPR compliance, overseeing data protection strategies, and acting as a point of contact for regulatory authorities and data subjects. This requirement helps businesses manage risks effectively while ensuring they handle personal data responsibly and transparently.

7. Cross-Border Data Transfers

Cross-border data transfers under the General Data Protection Regulation (GDPR) are subject to strict regulations to ensure that personal data leaving the European Union (EU) remains protected in accordance with EU privacy standards. Transfers of personal data from the EU to the United States are particularly scrutinized due to differences in data protection laws between the two regions. GDPR restricts such transfers unless adequate safeguards are in place to protect individuals' rights and freedoms. To facilitate compliance, U.S. entities must implement legally recognized mechanisms that ensure data protection is upheld even after the information is transferred out of the EU.

One of the most used mechanisms is the adoption of **Standard Contractual Clauses (SCCs)**, which are pre-approved legal agreements developed by the European Commission. These clauses require businesses to implement necessary safeguards to protect EU personal data and provide individuals with enforceable rights in the event of misuse. Another option is **Binding Corporate Rules (BCRs)**, which apply to multinational companies transferring data within their corporate group. BCRs require companies to establish internal policies that comply with GDPR's data protection principles and must be approved by EU supervisory authorities before implementation.

In addition to these contractual safeguards, businesses can comply with the GDPR's cross-border data transfer requirements by adhering to recognized frameworks that facilitate lawful data flows between the EU and the U.S. The **EU-U.S. Data Privacy Framework** (formerly known as the Privacy Shield) is one such arrangement that allows U.S. companies to self-certify compliance with specific data protection principles, ensuring an adequate level of security for EU personal data. However, previous iterations of such frameworks have faced legal challenges, with the **Privacy Shield being invalidated by the Court of Justice of the European Union in 2020** due to concerns over U.S. government surveillance practices. The revised Data Privacy Framework aims to address these concerns by introducing additional safeguards and oversight measures.

Failure to comply with GDPR's cross-border data transfer regulations can result in significant penalties, including fines of up to €20 million or 4% of a company's global annual revenue, whichever is higher. Non-compliance can also lead to restrictions on data transfers, operational disruptions, and reputational damage. Consequently, U.S. companies processing EU personal data must carefully evaluate their data transfer mechanisms, ensure legal compliance, and implement stringent safeguards to maintain trust and avoid legal repercussions.

8. Increased Operational Costs

Compliance with the General Data Protection Regulation (GDPR) often results in increased operational costs for businesses, particularly for U.S.

companies that process the personal data of EU residents. To meet GDPR's stringent requirements, organizations must invest in advanced data protection tools and infrastructure that enhance security, prevent breaches, and ensure lawful data processing. These investments may include encryption technologies, anonymization techniques, access control systems, and automated data management tools to handle user requests such as data access, rectification, and deletion efficiently. Companies must also implement monitoring and reporting mechanisms to detect and respond to security incidents promptly, reducing the risk of non-compliance and potential regulatory penalties.

Beyond technological upgrades, GDPR compliance necessitates hiring legal counsel or engaging data protection consultants to interpret the regulation's complex requirements and implement necessary policy changes. Many organizations appoint Data Protection Officers (DPOs) to oversee compliance efforts, ensure data protection impact assessments (DPIAs) are conducted when required, and serve as a liaison between the company and EU supervisory authorities. Additionally, companies must train employees on GDPR obligations, emphasizing best practices in data handling, breach response, and consumer rights management.

Another significant cost arises from updating contracts and agreements with vendors, partners, and third-party service providers to align with GDPR standards. Organizations that share or process personal data on behalf of others must ensure that data processing agreements (DPAs) are in place, outlining the responsibilities and liabilities of each party. This often requires renegotiating existing contracts, conducting compliance audits on vendors, and ensuring that third parties implement the necessary security measures to protect shared data.

Although GDPR compliance imposes substantial financial burdens, failure to adhere to its provisions can lead to far greater costs, including fines of up to €20 million or 4% of annual global revenue, legal disputes, and reputational damage. Many companies recognize that beyond regulatory adherence, robust data protection practices enhance customer trust and provide a competitive advantage in an increasingly privacy-conscious global market. As data privacy regulations continue to evolve worldwide, businesses that proactively invest in GDPR compliance position themselves for long-term operational resilience and credibility.

9. Liability and Fines

Non-compliance with GDPR can lead to **severe financial and reputational consequences** for businesses. Companies that fail to adhere to data protection regulations may face fines of up to **€20 million or 4% of their global annual revenue**, whichever is higher. Beyond financial penalties, businesses risk **losing customer trust and damaging their reputation**, as consumers are increasingly aware of and concerned about how their personal data is handled. A data breach or failure to comply with GDPR can lead to **negative publicity, legal challenges, and loss of business**, making compliance essential for any organization handling personal data.

10. Influence on U.S. Privacy Laws

The General Data Protection Regulation (GDPR) has had a significant impact on the evolution of privacy laws in the United States, influencing legislation at both the state and federal levels. While the U.S. has yet to implement a comprehensive federal data privacy law, GDPR's stringent requirements have set a global standard that many state laws have adopted to varying degrees. One of the most notable examples is the **California Consumer Privacy Act (CCPA)**, which was enacted in 2018 and shares several similarities with GDPR, including requirements for transparency, consumer data access rights, and restrictions on data sharing. The CCPA grants California residents the right to know what personal information businesses collect about them, the right to request deletion of their data, and the right to opt out of the sale of their information. These rights closely resemble GDPR's core principles, demonstrating how EU regulations have shaped privacy protections in the U.S.

Beyond California, other states, including **Virginia, Colorado, and Connecticut**, have enacted privacy laws that incorporate GDPR-like provisions. These laws require businesses to implement stronger data governance practices, enhance user consent mechanisms, and establish clear procedures for responding to consumer requests regarding their personal data. While these state laws are not identical to GDPR, their emphasis on consumer control and corporate accountability reflects the increasing importance of data privacy in the U.S. legal landscape.

For U.S. companies already compliant with GDPR, adapting to these emerging state privacy laws is often more straightforward, as many of the same principles—such as data minimization, security measures, and transparency—are integral to both frameworks. Businesses that have implemented GDPR-compliant policies, including detailed privacy notices, robust security controls, and mechanisms for handling data subject requests, find themselves in a stronger position to meet U.S. state law requirements with minimal additional effort.

The growing influence of GDPR on U.S. privacy legislation suggests a broader shift toward comprehensive data protection in the U.S. With increasing pressure for a **federal privacy law**, many industry experts anticipate that future U.S. regulations will draw heavily from GDPR principles. As more states implement their own privacy laws, companies operating across multiple jurisdictions must proactively enhance their data protection strategies to align with both U.S. and international standards. This alignment not only ensures compliance but also strengthens consumer trust, demonstrating a commitment to responsible data governance in an era of heightened privacy awareness.

Conclusion

The General Data Protection Regulation (GDPR), implemented by the European Union in 2018, has profoundly influenced data privacy practices worldwide, compelling U.S. businesses to reassess their data handling protocols. Given its extraterritorial scope, the GDPR mandates that any organization—regardless of geographic location—that offers goods or services to EU residents or monitors their behavior must comply with its stringent data protection standards. This requirement has led many U.S. companies to overhaul their data collection, processing, and storage methodologies to align with GDPR mandates.

Compliance necessitates several critical actions: obtaining explicit consent from users before data collection, ensuring transparent communication about data usage, and implementing robust security measures to protect personal information. Non-compliance carries the risk of substantial fines, which can reach up to €20 million or 4% of the company's global annual revenue, whichever is higher. This potential financial liability underscores the importance for U.S. businesses to prioritize GDPR adherence when engaging with EU markets.

Beyond legal obligations, the GDPR has set a global benchmark for data privacy, influencing legislation in various jurisdictions. For instance, the California Consumer Privacy Act (CCPA) reflects principles similar to those in the GDPR, indicating a broader shift towards enhanced consumer data protection in the U.S. This trend suggests that U.S. companies may benefit from adopting GDPR-compliant practices not only to facilitate international operations but also to anticipate and adapt to evolving domestic privacy regulations.

In summary, the GDPR's implementation has compelled U.S. businesses to critically evaluate and modify their data practices, ensuring they meet elevated standards of transparency, security, and user consent. This regulatory environment not only mitigates legal risks but also fosters greater consumer trust in an increasingly data-conscious global marketplace.

Chapter 5:
GDPR and Everyday Digital Life

GDPR has already influenced everyday digital life by setting higher standards for data privacy and security worldwide. Examining cases from the U.S. legal system where privacy was compromised helps highlight the importance of strong data protection regulations like GDPR.

Here are some examples from the U.S. legal system that highlight instances where individual privacy was compromised, along with the outcomes of those cases. These examples can be important to understand when discussing data privacy and the impact of regulations like GDPR.

1. Equifax Data Breach (2017)

Compromise: In 2017, Equifax, one of the largest credit reporting agencies in the U.S., announced a massive data breach that **exposed the personal information of approximately 147 million people**. The compromised data included Social Security numbers, names, addresses, credit card numbers, and other sensitive details1. The breach occurred due to a failure to patch a known vulnerability in Equifax's software1.

Outcome: The breach led to numerous class-action lawsuits and regulatory actions. **Equifax reached a**

settlement with the Federal Trade Commission (FTC) and 50 U.S. states, agreeing to pay up to $700 million in damages. As part of the settlement, Equifax was required to improve its data security practices and offer free credit monitoring services to affected individuals1.

The Equifax breach is a stark reminder that even large organizations entrusted with vast amounts of personal data can fail to protect it adequately. As the FTC emphasized, **companies must take reasonable steps to secure their systems**, or they will face serious consequences.

2. Facebook-Cambridge Analytica Scandal (2018)

Compromise: In 2018, it was revealed that **Cambridge Analytica, a political consulting firm, had harvested the personal data of millions of Facebook users without their consent.** The data was collected through a third-party app that users had downloaded, which then accessed not only the users' data but also the data of their friends. This information was then used for political advertising purposes1.

Outcome: The scandal led to significant public outcry and regulatory scrutiny. **Facebook faced investigations by the FTC and other regulatory bodies. In 2019, Facebook agreed to pay a $5 billion penalty to settle charges with the FTC for violating users' privacy.** The settlement also required Facebook to implement significant changes to its data governance practices and increase transparency.

The Cambridge Analytica scandal showed how easily personal data can be exploited for purposes users never intended. As regulators noted, **companies must be vigilant in ensuring that third-party apps do not abuse user data**, and they must be transparent about how data is being used.

3. Yahoo Data Breaches (2013-2014)

Compromise: Yahoo suffered multiple massive data breaches between 2013 and 2014, which **affected over 3 billion user accounts**. The compromised data included names, email addresses, passwords, security questions and answers, and dates of birth. The breaches were attributed to state-sponsored actors1.

Outcome: The breaches led to significant damage to Yahoo's reputation and affected its acquisition by Verizon. **Yahoo (later renamed Altaba) agreed to pay $117.5 million to settle a class-action lawsuit** brought by affected users. The settlement provided compensation for out-of-pocket expenses and time spent dealing with the breach. Additionally, Yahoo had to implement enhanced security measures1.

The Yahoo breaches underscore the persistent threat of cyberattacks and the importance of robust security measures. As security experts have pointed out, **companies must invest in protecting user data, or they risk losing not only money but also the trust of their customers**.

4. Target Data Breach (2013)

Compromise: In late 2013, **Target suffered a data breach that compromised the credit and debit card information of over 40 million customers**. Hackers gained access to Target's network through a third-party HVAC vendor and then installed malware on Target's point-of-sale (POS) systems1.

Outcome: The breach led to significant financial losses for Target and damaged its reputation. **Target reached a $18.5 million settlement with 47 states and the District of Columbia**. The settlement required Target to implement stronger security measures, including encryption of cardholder data and enhanced monitoring of its network.

The Target breach illustrates the vulnerability of retailers to cyberattacks and the importance of securing supply chains. As state attorneys general emphasized, **businesses must take responsibility for protecting consumer data**, and that includes ensuring their vendors have adequate security measures in place.

5. TCPA (Telephone Consumer Protection Act) Violations

Compromise: Companies that violate the TCPA by making unsolicited calls or sending texts without prior express consent risk lawsuits and penalties1.

Outcome: Penalties under the TCPA can be $500 to $1,500 per violation.

While the TCPA is not strictly a data breach issue, it highlights the importance of obtaining proper consent before contacting individuals. As legal experts note, **businesses must respect consumer preferences** and ensure they have explicit permission before engaging in marketing communications.

These cases highlight the various ways in which individual privacy can be compromised and the potential consequences for both individuals and organizations. They underscore the importance of strong data protection measures and the need for regulatory oversight to ensure accountability.

In today's world, it feels like our lives are completely intertwined with the digital space. We shop online, book doctor's appointments through apps, check our kids' grades on a school portal, and share photos with family members through social media platforms. But with all the convenience comes a question: **How safe is your data? General Data Protection Regulation (GDPR)**, the European law that's making waves across the globe, and how it impacts **your everyday life**. Well, this chapter is all about that—how GDPR is shaping the way we interact with our favorite apps, websites, and services in our daily routines, and how it's giving you more control over your personal information.

Scenario 1: Your Favorite Shopping Website Knows You already

Imagine you're browsing your favorite online store on a Saturday afternoon, searching for a new winter jacket. Suddenly, the website suggests the exact style you were considering, conveniently in your size. How does it know? **Before GDPR**, websites could track your online activity—what you viewed, clicked on, or even left in your cart—without your knowledge. This data was often used for targeted advertising and, in some cases, sold to third parties without your consent. **Under GDPR**, businesses must now be transparent about data collection. When you visit a website, they are required to **ask for your consent** before collecting browsing data, **explain how your data will be used**, and **allow you to opt out or delete your information** if you no longer want it stored. This gives consumers more control over their personal data, ensuring that if they are uncomfortable with tracking, they can refuse or revoke permission at any time.

A similar scenario plays out with **fitness tracking apps**. Before GDPR, an app might have collected detailed health and activity data—like your steps, heart rate, and workout habits—without explicitly informing you where that data was stored or how it was shared. Some companies even sold this data to insurers or advertisers. **Now, under GDPR,** fitness apps must clearly disclose their data usage policies, obtain user consent before collecting sensitive health information, and provide options to delete stored data upon request. These protections ensure that consumers have a **clear choice** about how their data is handled, reinforcing trust and security in digital services.

Scenario 2: Your Kid's School Portal Shares Data with Third Parties

Imagine you're using a school app to track your child's grades, assignments, and teacher communications. One day, you receive an email from a company offering discounts on school supplies, leaving you wondering—**how did they get your email? Before GDPR,** schools or their vendors might have shared your personal information, including your email or even details about your child's academic performance, with third-party advertisers without informing you. This data sharing often happened behind the scenes, with little to no oversight from parents. **Under GDPR,** schools must now **ask for explicit consent** before sharing student or parent data, **be transparent** about how the information is used, who has access to it, and how long it is stored, and **allow parents to withdraw consent or delete their data** if they no longer want it shared. This ensures that families have control over their personal information and can prevent unauthorized data sharing.

A similar scenario can occur with **smart home devices,** such as voice assistants or security cameras. Many families use these devices for convenience and safety, but **before GDPR,** some manufacturers collected and stored user data—like voice recordings, usage patterns, or even video footage—without clearly disclosing how it was used. Some companies even **shared or sold** this data to third-party advertisers or analytics firms. **Now, under GDPR,** companies must **obtain user consent** before collecting personal data, **explain how it will be used and stored,** and **offer options to delete recordings or personal information upon request.** This regulation helps ensure that even in the digital home environment, individuals have greater control over how their private data is handled and shared.

Scenario 3: Social Media Apps Show Ads Based on What You Post

You're scrolling through your social media feed when, out of nowhere, an ad for a yoga mat appears. You haven't searched for one, but you recently posted photos from a yoga class. Before GDPR, social media platforms and other apps could freely collect data from your posts, likes, and interactions to build a profile of your interests. This information was then used to serve you personalized ads—often without your knowledge or consent. Under GDPR, social media companies must now obtain explicit consent before using your data for targeted advertising. They must also be transparent about what information they collect, such as your posts, photos, and interactions, and explain whether it's used for advertising, app improvements, or other purposes. Additionally, users now have the right to access, modify, or delete their data if they no longer want platforms storing their preferences or personal information.

A similar situation can happen with smartphone apps that access your microphone or location data. Have you ever had a conversation about a product, only to see an ad for it shortly afterward? Before GDPR, many apps could access your microphone or track your location in the background, sometimes without clearly informing you. This data was often shared with advertisers to deliver highly personalized ads. Now, under GDPR, apps must explicitly ask for permission before collecting sensitive data, such as microphone access or location tracking. Users must also be given the option to review, limit, or revoke these permissions at any time. These protections help ensure that individuals have control over how their digital footprint is used, preventing companies from exploiting personal data without consent.

Scenario 4: You Share Personal Information with an Online Fitness App

You sign up for a fitness app to track your workouts and receive meal suggestions based on your health data. After a few months, you start receiving emails recommending health supplements, even though you never searched for them. Before GDPR, fitness apps could collect and share sensitive health data—such as workout routines, weight, and dietary preferences—with third-party companies, often without informing users. This data was commonly used for targeted advertising, with little transparency about how it was being stored or shared. Under GDPR, fitness apps must now obtain explicit consent before collecting or sharing sensitive data related to health or fitness. They must also clearly disclose how the data is being used, whether it's for app improvements, advertising, or personalized product recommendations. Additionally, users have the right to control, delete, or modify their data whenever they choose, ensuring they remain in charge of their personal information.

A similar scenario can occur with mental health and wellness apps. Many people use meditation, therapy, or stress-relief apps that track emotions, moods, or even journal entries. Before GDPR, some of these apps could share user data with advertisers or insurance companies without consent, potentially impacting things like insurance eligibility. Now, under GDPR, these apps must explicitly ask for permission before collecting or sharing such deeply personal data. They must also provide users with the ability to opt-out of data tracking, delete stored information, and understand exactly how their data is being used. This ensures that even highly sensitive personal data is handled responsibly, giving individuals greater control over their privacy.

In today's digital world, nearly every aspect of life is connected to online services. From shopping and banking to social media, healthcare, and education, personal data is continuously being collected and used by companies. While these digital interactions provide convenience, they also raise concerns about privacy and security. The General Data Protection Regulation (GDPR), a European Union law, aims to address these concerns by giving individuals more control over their personal information and ensuring businesses handle data responsibly. GDPR has not only influenced European companies but has also shaped global data protection practices, affecting individuals worldwide.

How GDPR Impacts Everyday Digital Interactions

GDPR enforces transparency in how businesses collect, store, and use personal data. When you browse an online store, GDPR mandates that businesses ask for explicit consent before tracking your activity. If a company collects data for targeted advertising, it must inform users and provide an option to opt out. This level of transparency ensures that individuals can decide whether they want to share their information or keep it private.

For example, before GDPR, online retailers would track customer behavior without consent, storing browsing history and preferences to create personalized advertisements. Now, they must obtain permission before collecting such data and allow users to request deletion if they no longer wish to be tracked. Similarly, schools and educational platforms that store student data must obtain parental consent before sharing information with third-party vendors. Parents can also request the removal of their child's data if they no longer want it stored.

Social media platforms, which previously used personal data for targeted advertising without user awareness, must now be transparent about what data they collect and how it is used. If a user posts about fitness activities, for example, they may receive ads for workout equipment. However, under GDPR, platforms must explicitly ask for consent to use posts and interactions for advertising purposes. Users also have the right to delete their data or modify their preferences at any time.

Healthcare and fitness applications must comply with GDPR by obtaining explicit consent before collecting sensitive health-related data. Whether it's a fitness app tracking workouts or a telemedicine service storing medical records, GDPR ensures that users are informed about how their data is being used. Companies cannot share this data with third parties without clear consent, and users have the right to control or delete their information whenever they choose.

Key Areas Where GDPR Affects Users

GDPR impacts various aspects of digital life by giving users more control over their personal data. In **online shopping**, websites must obtain user consent before tracking browsing habits for personalized marketing, and consumers can opt out of data collection or request their information be deleted. **Social media platforms** must be transparent about the data they collect, allowing users to access, modify, or remove their personal information whenever they choose. **Healthcare and fitness apps** are required to obtain explicit consent before collecting or sharing sensitive health data, ensuring users retain full control over their medical and fitness information. In **educational settings**, schools must seek parental permission before sharing student data with third-party services, and parents have the right to request the removal of their child's personal information. Additionally, **email subscriptions and newsletters** must clearly inform users about the type of data being collected and how it will be used, while also providing an easy way to opt out. These regulations ensure greater privacy and security for individuals, making businesses more accountable for handling personal data responsibly.

Enhancing Consumer Rights and Security

Beyond data transparency, GDPR enhances consumer rights by allowing individuals to access and manage their personal information. Users can request copies of their stored data, verify its accuracy, and demand corrections or deletions when necessary. The "Right to Be Forgotten" ensures that individuals can have their data erased from a company's records if they no longer wish to engage with a service.

Another crucial aspect of GDPR is data portability, which enables users to transfer their information from one service provider to another without difficulty. This is particularly useful when switching email providers, social networks, or digital banking services.

GDPR also enforces strict security measures to protect sensitive data. Companies handling health, financial, or biometric information must implement robust safeguards to prevent unauthorized access and breaches. If a data breach occurs, businesses are required to notify both the authorities and affected individuals within 72 hours, ensuring swift action to minimize harm.

Impact on Businesses and Future Trends

Businesses worldwide have had to adjust their practices to comply with GDPR. Companies operating in the EU, or dealing with EU citizens' data, must ensure they follow these regulations or risk substantial fines. Many organizations outside the EU have also adopted GDPR-like standards, recognizing that stronger data protection builds consumer trust.

Looking ahead, GDPR continues to set the benchmark for data privacy laws globally. Its influence has led to the creation of similar laws in other countries, including the California Consumer Privacy Act (CCPA) in the United States. As digital interactions expand, GDPR's principles will likely continue shaping the future of online privacy and data protection.

Conclusion: Taking Control of Your Data

GDPR is more than just a regulation; it is a framework designed to empower individuals in the digital age. By ensuring transparency, security, and accountability, it allows users to take control of their personal data. Whether shopping online, engaging on social media, using fitness apps, or managing school and healthcare records, individuals now can decide how their information is collected and used. As digital technology continues to evolve, GDPR remains a critical tool in safeguarding privacy and promoting responsible data handling across industries.

Chapter 6:
GDPR's Notification Obligations

(What Happens When Your Data Is Breached?)

When personal data is compromised or exposed in a data breach, the General Data Protection Regulation (GDPR) enforces strict notification obligations to ensure transparency and accountability. Organizations that process the personal data of individuals within the European Union (EU) are required to follow specific protocols when a breach occurs, regardless of where the company is based. These obligations are particularly relevant for American users interacting with services that collect European customer data, as well as for businesses that manage sensitive personal information. Understanding these requirements is crucial in both personal and professional contexts, as failure to comply with GDPR's notification mandates can result in severe penalties and reputational damage.

Under GDPR, organizations must notify the relevant supervisory authority within **72 hours** of becoming aware of a data breach unless it is unlikely to result in a risk to individuals' rights and freedoms. This notification must include essential details such as the nature of the breach, the categories of data affected, the approximate number of individuals impacted, and the steps being taken to mitigate the damage. If the breach poses a **high risk** to individuals, organizations are also required to inform the affected individuals **without undue delay**. This ensures that users can take necessary precautions, such as changing passwords, monitoring their financial activity, or being aware of potential identity theft risks.

For businesses operating in the U.S. that handle EU customer data, these requirements underscore the importance of having a well-structured data protection and breach response strategy. Companies must implement proactive security measures such as encryption, access controls, and continuous monitoring to minimize the likelihood of breaches. Additionally, they must have clear protocols in place to detect breaches quickly, assess their severity, and communicate effectively with both regulators and affected individuals. Failure to comply with GDPR's breach notification requirements can result in significant fines, reaching up to **€10 million or 2% of a company's annual global revenue**, whichever is higher. In cases of severe non-compliance, penalties can be even more substantial.

Ultimately, GDPR's notification obligations serve to protect individuals by ensuring they are promptly informed when their personal data has been compromised. These regulations also push businesses to maintain high security standards, fostering a culture of accountability in the handling of personal information. Whether as a consumer or a business professional, understanding these obligations is essential in today's digital landscape, where data breaches are increasingly common, and privacy concerns continue to grow.

Let's break it down in simple terms so you understand how **GDPR**'s notification rules apply to your daily life.

Understanding GDPR's Notification Obligations and How They Impact You

The General Data Protection Regulation (GDPR) has established clear notification requirements for companies that collect or store personal data in the event of a data breach. These regulations ensure that affected individuals are informed promptly, allowing them to take necessary actions to protect themselves from identity theft, fraud, or other potential harm. If a company fails to comply with GDPR's notification obligations, it can face severe financial penalties and damage to its reputation. Whether you are an American consumer using services that process EU data, a business professional handling customer information, or a healthcare provider managing sensitive patient records, understanding these obligations is crucial in today's data-driven world.

The GDPR Notification Process: What Happens When Your Data is Breached?

When a data breach occurs, the affected company is required to act swiftly. First, the organization must **immediately assess the breach** to determine the nature and extent of the data exposure. This includes identifying what personal data has been compromised, how it was accessed, and whether the breach poses a significant risk to individuals. Within **72 hours**, the company must notify the relevant Data Protection Authority (DPA) in the affected EU country, providing details about the breach, its potential impact, and the measures being taken to mitigate damage. Failure to meet this deadline can result in financial penalties, with fines reaching up to €10 million or 2% of a company's global annual revenue.

If the breach is likely to result in **high risk to individuals' privacy**, such as exposing sensitive personal data (e.g., financial information, health records, or login credentials), the company must **directly inform affected individuals** without undue delay. This notification may be delivered through email, phone calls, or public announcements on the company's website, ensuring that customers are aware of the risks. The notification must include clear details about **what happened, what data was exposed, what steps the company is taking to address the issue, and what individuals can do to protect themselves**. Organizations must also ensure that affected individuals have access to additional support, such as identity theft protection or fraud monitoring services.

Real-Life Scenario: GDPR in Action

Consider a scenario where you sign up for a fitness and health tracking app that stores your personal information, including medical history, exercise habits, and biometric data. If this company experiences a security breach, allowing hackers to access user data, GDPR requires the company to take immediate action. Within 72 hours, it must notify the appropriate EU regulatory body and assess whether the breach poses a risk to individuals. If the exposed data includes sensitive health records that could be misused for identity theft or insurance fraud, the company must notify affected users as soon as possible. You would receive an email or a message informing you about **what happened, what information was accessed, and what steps you should take, such as changing passwords or monitoring your medical records for suspicious activity**.

Could You Be Affected by a Data Breach?

With digital services becoming an integral part of daily life, it is essential to evaluate your exposure to potential data breaches. If you use online platforms that collect personal data—such as shopping websites, healthcare apps, or social media networks—you may be vulnerable. Additionally, if you frequently share sensitive information online, such as payment details or medical records, you should be aware of the risks associated with breaches. If you have ever received a notification from a company about a data breach, it is crucial to follow their recommended steps to secure your information and minimize potential harm.

How GDPR's Notification Rules Affect U.S. Households, Workers, and Professionals

While GDPR is an EU regulation, it has a significant impact on U.S. individuals and businesses that interact with EU-based services or collect data from EU residents. **For households**, parents using online platforms for their children must be aware of how these services handle personal information and whether they provide breach notifications in case of data exposure. If a family's health records are stored in a healthcare app or an online medical service, they should ensure that the provider follows proper security measures and has a clear process for notifying users in case of a breach.

For employees working in businesses that process personal data, GDPR's breach notification requirements may directly affect daily operations. Workers in customer service, IT security, or data management roles might be responsible for reporting breaches, handling customer inquiries about exposed data, or ensuring that internal breach response protocols are followed. Businesses must have an incident response plan that outlines how to notify both regulatory authorities and affected customers to maintain compliance and trust.

For healthcare professionals, GDPR's breach notification rules are similar to the U.S.'s **Health Insurance Portability and Accountability Act (HIPAA)**, which also mandates timely notifications when protected health information (PHI) is compromised. If a medical provider or insurance company experiences a data breach involving patient records, they must inform affected individuals and regulators, ensuring that proper precautions are taken to prevent misuse of the exposed data.

Consequences of Failing to Notify Individuals in Time

Companies that fail to comply with GDPR's notification requirements face severe penalties. If an organization does not report a data breach within the 72-hour timeframe, it could be fined up to €10 million or 2% of its annual global revenue. If a company neglects to notify affected individuals in a timely manner, particularly in cases where their personal data is at risk, fines could be even higher. Beyond financial repercussions, failing to act transparently can damage a company's reputation, leading to loss of consumer trust and potential legal action from affected individuals.

What Should You Do If You Receive a Breach Notification?

If you receive a notification informing you that your personal data has been compromised, it is essential to take immediate action to secure your information. **First, carefully review the notification** to understand what data was exposed and what risks you may face. The company should clearly explain whether login credentials, financial details, or sensitive personal records were affected.

Next, take proactive steps to protect yourself. If the breach involved login credentials, change your passwords immediately and enable two-factor authentication on affected accounts. If financial data was compromised, monitor your bank statements and credit reports for unusual activity. If you suspect identity theft, report it to the relevant authorities and freeze your credit to prevent fraudulent transactions. Companies often provide affected individuals with fraud monitoring services or security updates—follow their advice to minimize potential risks.

In the digital age, data breaches have become an unfortunate reality. GDPR's notification obligations exist to protect individuals by ensuring that they receive timely information when their personal data is exposed. Whether you are a consumer, a business professional, or a healthcare provider, understanding these rules can help you respond effectively in the event of a breach, safeguard sensitive information, and hold companies accountable for the security of your personal data.

Summary

The General Data Protection Regulation (GDPR) establishes strict notification obligations to ensure that individuals are promptly informed when their personal data has been compromised in a breach. These requirements are essential for safeguarding privacy and preventing risks such as identity theft, financial fraud, and unauthorized access to sensitive information. When a data breach occurs, companies are required to act swiftly by assessing the extent of the breach, notifying the appropriate data protection authorities within 72 hours, and informing affected individuals if the breach poses a significant risk to their rights and freedoms. Transparency and timely communication are fundamental principles under GDPR, ensuring that individuals have the necessary information to take precautionary measures, such as changing passwords, monitoring their financial transactions, or securing their personal accounts.

For consumers, employees, and patients, understanding these notification rules is vital in maintaining control over personal data. Individuals should be aware of their rights under GDPR, including the right to be informed when their data has been exposed and the steps they can take to mitigate potential harm. If a company fails to notify affected individuals in a timely manner, or if an individual suspects mishandling of personal information, they have the right to report the issue to regulatory authorities and seek legal recourse.

As GDPR places significant responsibility on businesses, organizations must prioritize strong security measures to prevent data breaches from occurring in the first place. The next chapter will explore the essential security requirements that companies must implement to ensure compliance with GDPR and protect user data from unauthorized access or cyber threats. By understanding both the notification obligations and preventive security measures, businesses and individuals alike can play a proactive role in strengthening data privacy in the digital age.

How GDPR Impacts U.S. Healthcare and HIPAA-Covered Entities

In an era where digital health services are expanding rapidly, privacy regulations like the General Data Protection Regulation (GDPR) and the Health

Insurance Portability and Accountability Act (HIPAA) play a crucial role in safeguarding personal health data. While HIPAA primarily applies to healthcare providers and insurers in the United States, GDPR extends its protections globally, impacting U.S. businesses that handle the personal data of European patients or work with European healthcare entities. Understanding how GDPR affects U.S. healthcare operations is vital for patients, providers, and business owners navigating digital health services.

Using a Health App to Monitor Symptoms

Imagine a parent downloading a health tracking app to monitor their child's cough symptoms. The app requests information such as the child's age, symptoms, and medication history. Prior to GDPR, such an app could collect this data without informing the user of its intended use, potentially sharing it with third-party advertisers. Now, under GDPR, the app must obtain explicit consent before gathering health-related data. It must also clearly state how the data will be used, whether for symptom analysis, product recommendations, or research. Additionally, users have the right to request the deletion of their data at any time, ensuring greater control over their personal health information.

Doctor's Offices and Third-Party Marketing

In a traditional healthcare setting, a patient visiting a family doctor might provide an email address during registration. WIthout clear regulations, the doctor's office could have shared that email and health history with marketing companies, resulting in targeted health-related advertisements without the patient's knowledge. GDPR requires healthcare providers to seek explicit permission before sharing any personal information with third parties. Additionally, patients must be informed about how their data will be used and given the option to opt out of marketing communications. This ensures that patients maintain full control over how their health data is utilized outside of direct medical care.

Health Insurance Companies and Cross-Border Data Sharing

For individuals using health insurance services, particularly those with international coverage, concerns about cross-border data sharing are growing. A U.S.-based insurance company partnering with European healthcare providers must comply with GDPR regulations when handling European patient data. Before GDPR, an insurer might have shared patient data with overseas partners without informing policyholders. Now, if an insurance provider works with European entities, it must adhere to GDPR standards, offering policyholders transparency regarding who has access to their data. Policyholders also have the right to request access to their information and can demand its deletion if they no longer wish to have it stored.

Telemedicine and Small Healthcare Businesses

For small healthcare providers and clinics expanding into telemedicine, GDPR compliance becomes a critical factor when serving European patients. A U.S.-based healthcare provider offering virtual consultations to European residents must ensure they follow GDPR's strict guidelines on data handling. This includes obtaining consent before collecting patient health data, implementing secure storage methods such as encryption, and providing the ability for patients to request data deletion or anonymization. Without proper data protection measures, providers risk non-compliance penalties and potential loss of trust from international patients.

The Broader Impact of GDPR on U.S. Healthcare

For U.S. healthcare professionals, patients, and business owners, GDPR introduces an added layer of protection that aligns with HIPAA's goal of safeguarding health information. While HIPAA regulates U.S. healthcare providers and insurers, GDPR ensures that individuals interacting with international health services receive similar protections. Whether tracking symptoms through a health app, receiving care from an international provider, or managing patient data as a healthcare professional, GDPR reinforces the importance of consent, transparency, and data security.

Conclusion: Navigating GDPR and HIPAA for a Secure Digital Health Future

GDPR and HIPAA work together to give individuals greater control over their health data, ensuring privacy protections that extend beyond national borders. By complying with GDPR, U.S. businesses that handle European patient data can align with global privacy standards while continuing to provide digital healthcare services securely. Whether as a parent managing their child's medical data, a healthcare provider adopting telemedicine, or an insurance company handling international claims, understanding and implementing GDPR principles ensures a more transparent and secure digital health environment. By integrating GDPR into everyday healthcare operations, we move toward a future where health data remains private, secure, and firmly under individual control.

Penalties and Enforcement

(What Happens if Data Protection Laws Are Broken?)

Data protection laws like the General Data Protection Regulation (GDPR) and the Health Insurance Portability and Accountability Act (HIPAA) exist to safeguard personal and health-related data. When businesses, healthcare providers, or other organizations fail to comply with these regulations, penalties are enforced to hold them accountable and ensure individuals' rights are protected. These penalties serve as a deterrent, compelling organizations to take data privacy seriously. Whether you are a consumer, healthcare patient, or business owner, understanding how these penalties work can help you stay informed and act if your rights are violated.

GDPR Penalties and Enforcement

GDPR applies to businesses worldwide that process the personal data of European Union (EU) citizens, regardless of where the company is based. Its penalties for non-compliance are among the toughest in data protection laws, with fines reaching up to **€20 million or 4% of a company's annual global revenue**, whichever is higher. These fines are categorized based on the severity of the violation. **Minor violations**, such as failing to implement adequate data security measures, can result in fines of up to **€10 million or 2% of global revenue**. More **serious breaches**, like processing personal data without consent or unlawfully sharing user information, can lead to the maximum penalties. For example, if a U.S.-based online retailer collects customer emails and sells them to third-party advertisers without permission, GDPR could impose substantial fines, forcing the business to change its data-handling practices. These strict regulations encourage companies to adopt **stronger privacy measures**, ensuring that personal data is handled **transparently and securely**.

Notable GDPR Violation Cases

Several high-profile companies have faced substantial fines under GDPR for failing to protect user data. Some key cases include:

1. **Meta (Facebook)** – In May 2023, Meta was fined €1.2 billion by the Irish Data Protection Commission for transferring European user

data to the U.S. without sufficient protection mechanisms.

2. **TikTok** – In September 2023, TikTok was fined €345 million for violating GDPR regulations concerning children's data, including default public account settings for minors.

3. **Uber** – In August 2024, Uber was fined €290 million for transferring European driver data to the U.S. without appropriate safeguards.

4. **Google** – In December 2021, Google was fined €90 million for making it more difficult for users to reject cookies than to accept them, violating GDPR's transparency requirements.

5. **Enel Energia SpA** – In February 2024, the Italian data authority fined the energy company €79.10 million for failing to implement adequate data security measures.

These cases highlight the significant financial and operational consequences of GDPR non-compliance and the importance of robust data protection strategies.

Smaller Companies and GDPR Compliance

GDPR enforcement extends beyond major corporations. Small businesses have also been fined for violations, such as:

- **Tax Return Limited** – Fined €200,000 for sending unsolicited marketing messages without user consent.

- **DM Design Bedrooms Ltd.** – Fined €160,000 for making millions of unauthorized marketing calls.
- **Lifestyle Marketing, Mother & Baby Ltd.** – Fined €140,000 for reselling personal information without obtaining consent.

These cases demonstrate that GDPR enforcement is not exclusive to large enterprises; smaller businesses must also comply with data protection laws to avoid severe fines and reputational damage.

Comparison of GDPR and CCPA Penalties

In addition to GDPR, the California Consumer Privacy Act (CCPA) enforces data privacy regulations in the U.S. Some key differences between the two laws include:

- **Fines and Penalties:** GDPR imposes severe penalties, with fines reaching up to €20 million or 4% of global annual revenue, whereas CCPA fines range from $2,500 per unintentional violation to $7,500 per intentional violation.
- **Enforcement Authorities:** GDPR is enforced by national data protection authorities in each EU member state, while CCPA enforcement falls under the California Attorney General and the California Privacy Protection Agency (CPPA).
- **Breach Notification:** GDPR requires businesses to report breaches within 72 hours, while CCPA

mandates notification "in the most expedient time possible."

- **Private Right of Action:** GDPR allows individuals to lodge complaints with regulatory bodies, whereas CCPA enables consumers to file lawsuits for specific violations, particularly data breaches.

HIPAA Penalties and Enforcement

HIPAA governs the confidentiality of health information in the U.S., imposing penalties on healthcare providers and insurers that fail to protect patient data. The penalties vary based on the level of negligence:

- **Tier 1 (Unknowing Violations):** Up to $50,000 per violation, with a maximum annual penalty of $1.5 million.
- **Tier 2 (Reasonable Cause):** Fines range from $1,000 to $50,000 per violation.
- **Tier 3 (Willful Neglect, Corrected):** Penalties range from $10,000 to $50,000 per violation if corrective action is taken.
- **Tier 4 (Willful Neglect, Not Corrected):** Fines reach $50,000 per violation, with an annual maximum of $1.5 million.

For example, if a hospital mistakenly sends patient records to the wrong insurance company, it could be classified as a Tier 1 violation, whereas a provider ignoring repeated warnings about security risks could face Tier 4 penalties.

Life Scenarios: How These Laws Affect You

To illustrate how these penalties apply in real life, consider the following scenarios:

- **Online Data Misuse:** A shopping website collects and shares your personal data without consent, violating GDPR. The company faces significant fines and must update its privacy policies.
- **Healthcare Data Breach:** Your doctor accidentally shares your medical records with an incorrect third party. Under HIPAA, the healthcare provider is fined for the unauthorized disclosure of patient information.
- **U.S. Company Serving EU Customers:** A fitness app collects sensitive health data and shares it with advertisers without consent. GDPR enforcement results in heavy fines, forcing the company to revise its data-handling practices.

Why You Should Care About Data Protection Penalties

Organizations that handle sensitive personal data must follow strict regulations to prevent misuse, data breaches, and unauthorized access. When they fail to do so, enforcement mechanisms ensure they face **serious consequences**, including heavy fines and legal actions. These penalties serve two key purposes: they **encourage businesses to adopt secure data practices** and provide consumers with a way to seek justice if their personal information is mishandled. Whether it's an **online retailer selling your data without consent** or a **healthcare provider exposing your medical records**, you have rights under these regulations to take action.

Understanding the penalties for data breaches helps individuals recognize their rights and respond appropriately if their personal data is compromised. These regulations not only **protect consumers from privacy violations** but also **hold businesses accountable**, pushing them to implement stronger security measures. When companies risk **significant fines for mishandling data**, they are more likely to prioritize data protection and transparency. This ultimately creates a safer digital environment where individuals have greater control over their personal information.

What You Can Do if Your Data Rights Are Violated

If you believe your data privacy has been compromised, there are several steps you can take depending on the law that applies to your situation. **For GDPR violations**, you can **file a complaint** with the relevant **EU Data Protection Authority (DPA)** or request access to your personal data to see how it has been used. **For HIPAA violations**, such as unauthorized access to your medical records, you can **report the issue** to the **Office for Civil Rights (OCR)** and request a copy of your health information to ensure it has been handled properly. **For CCPA violations**, which apply to California residents, you can

contact the California Privacy Protection Agency or pursue **legal action** if your data was exposed in a breach. Knowing your rights under these laws empowers you to take action and hold organizations accountable for protecting your personal information.

Conclusion

The enforcement of GDPR, HIPAA, and other privacy regulations ensures that businesses and healthcare providers handle personal data responsibly. These laws establish strict penalties for non-compliance, encouraging organizations to prioritize data security and transparency. By understanding these regulations, individuals can better protect their data, exercise their rights, and hold organizations accountable for privacy violations. In the next chapter, we will explore how businesses can ensure compliance with GDPR and HIPAA to prevent violations before they occur.

Part 3: GDPR and it's Equivalents in USA

GDPR equivalents in USA

In the United States, there is no single federal equivalent to the General Data Protection Regulation (GDPR), which is the comprehensive data protection law in the European Union. However, several state laws and federal regulations address similar privacy concerns in specific contexts. Below are some U.S. equivalents or analogous frameworks:

Federal Privacy Regulations

1. **Health Insurance Portability and Accountability Act (HIPAA)**
   - Protects health information in the healthcare and insurance sectors.
   - Applies to covered entities like healthcare providers, health plans, and business associates.
2. **Children's Online Privacy Protection Act (COPPA)**
   - Regulates the collection of personal data from children under 13 years old by online services and websites.
3. **Gramm-Leach-Bliley Act (GLBA)**
   - Applies to financial institutions and focuses on safeguarding sensitive financial information.
4. **Federal Trade Commission (FTC) Act**
   - Empowers the FTC to act against unfair or deceptive practices, including privacy violations.

State-Level Privacy Laws

1. **California Consumer Privacy Act (CCPA)/ California Privacy Rights Act (CPRA)**
    - Closest equivalent to GDPR in the U.S.
    - Gives California residents rights such as access, deletion, and opting out of the sale of their personal data.
    - Introduces concepts like data minimization and processing restrictions like GDPR.
2. **Virginia Consumer Data Protection Act (VCDPA)**
    - Offers rights like data access, correction, and deletion for Virginia residents.
    - Establishes requirements for data protection assessments and opt-out rights for targeted advertising.
3. **Colorado Privacy Act (CPA)**
    - Mirrors many GDPR principles, providing residents with rights over their personal data and requiring companies to implement data protection measures.
4. **Connecticut and Utah Privacy Laws**
    - Recently enacted privacy laws offering residents certain rights and imposing data processing obligations on companies.

Key Differences from GDPR

Privacy laws in the U.S. differ significantly from the **General Data Protection Regulation (GDPR)** in both scope and enforcement. **GDPR applies broadly** to any organization, regardless of location, if it processes the personal data of **EU residents**. In contrast, U.S. privacy laws are often **sector-specific** (such as HIPAA for healthcare or COPPA for children's online data) or **state-specific** (such as the CCPA in California or the VCDPA in Virginia). This means that while GDPR offers a **comprehensive framework** for data protection, U.S. regulations tend to **apply only in certain industries or regions**.

Another key difference is the **legal basis for processing data**. Under GDPR, organizations must have a **lawful reason** to collect and process personal data, such as user consent, contractual necessity, or legitimate business interests. U.S. laws, however, typically focus on **notice and consent**, requiring businesses to inform users about data collection but often **allowing data use unless the consumer explicitly opts out**. For example, the **California Consumer Privacy Act (CCPA)** and similar laws in **Virginia (VCDPA), Colorado (CPA), Connecticut, and Utah** require businesses to provide **opt-out mechanisms** for data sharing, but they do not impose GDPR-style restrictions on processing without a legal basis.

Penalties for non-compliance also differ significantly. **GDPR enforces strict financial penalties**, with fines reaching up to **€20 million or 4% of a company's global turnover**, making non-compliance a serious risk. U.S. laws impose **varying penalties**, often **lower and less uniform**. For instance, **HIPAA** violations in healthcare can result in hefty fines, while **COPPA** enforces penalties for companies collecting children's data without parental consent. The **Gramm-Leach-Bliley Act (GLBA)** governs financial data but primarily requires disclosure rather than restricting data use. The **Federal Trade Commission (FTC)** also plays a role in **enforcing privacy violations**, particularly in cases of deceptive or unfair practices, but it does not have a dedicated, overarching privacy law like GDPR.

Overall, **GDPR offers a more unified and stringent approach to data privacy**, while the **U.S. relies on a patchwork of sector-based and state-level regulations**. This creates **inconsistencies in consumer protections**, with some states offering stronger privacy rights than others, and businesses facing **different compliance requirements depending on where they operate**.

Emerging Trends

In recent years, there has been a significant push towards establishing a comprehensive federal privacy law in the United States. Despite multiple legislative efforts, including the introduction of the American Data Privacy and Protection Act (ADPPA) and the American Privacy Rights Act (APRA), consensus in Congress remains elusive. Key sticking points include debates over federal preemption of existing state laws and the extent of enforcement mechanisms, such as private rights of action. As a result, the U.S. continues to operate without a unified federal privacy standard, leading to a complex landscape of state-specific regulations.

The absence of federal legislation has prompted individual states to take matters into their own hands, leading to a proliferation of state-level privacy laws. As of September 2024, twenty states, including California, Virginia, and Colorado, have enacted comprehensive data privacy statutes. Many of these laws draw inspiration from California's pioneering Consumer Privacy Act (CCPA) and its subsequent amendment, the California Privacy Rights Act (CPRA). While these state laws share common themes, such as granting consumers rights over their personal data and imposing obligations on businesses regarding data handling practices, they also exhibit critical differences. Variations exist in definitions, scope, and specific consumer rights, creating a patchwork regulatory environment that poses significant compliance challenges for businesses operating across multiple jurisdictions.

The current situation underscores the urgent need for a cohesive federal privacy framework. A unified law would provide consistent protections for consumers nationwide and offer businesses a clear set of standards to follow, reducing the complexity and potential conflicts arising from the existing mosaic of state regulations. Until such federal legislation is enacted, companies must navigate the intricate and evolving landscape of state privacy laws, ensuring compliance with each jurisdiction's unique requirements to mitigate legal risks and protect consumer trust.

Chapter 7:
How GDPR Compares to CCPA

The **General Data Protection Regulation (GDPR)** and the **California Consumer Privacy Act (CCPA)** are two significant data privacy laws, but they differ in scope, application, and requirements. Here's a comparison to clarify their key similarities and differences:

1. Scope of Application

The **General Data Protection Regulation (GDPR)** and the **California Consumer Privacy Act (CCPA)** both aim to protect personal data but differ in scope and applicability. GDPR applies globally to any organization that processes the personal data of EU residents, regardless of the company's location or size. It covers a broad range of personal data, including names, emails, IP addresses, and biometric data, and imposes strict obligations such as obtaining explicit consent, ensuring data portability, and appointing Data Protection Officers (DPOs) when required. Non-compliance can result in fines of up to €20 million or 4% of global revenue, making GDPR one of the most stringent data protection laws worldwide.

In contrast, CCPA is a state-specific law that applies only to for-profit businesses operating in California that meet certain thresholds, such as annual revenue exceeding $25 million, handling data from 100,000 or more consumers, or deriving 50% or more of revenue from selling personal data. It focuses on consumer rights, allowing California residents to access, delete, and opt out of the sale of their data. Unlike GDPR, CCPA does not require appointing a DPO or conducting Data Protection Impact Assessments (DPIAs), but it does require businesses to provide clear notices about data collection. Non-compliance can result in civil penalties enforced by the California Attorney General and statutory damages in cases of data breaches.

Overall, GDPR is a broad, global privacy law centered on individual rights and strict compliance measures, while CCPA is more focused on consumer empowerment and transparency within California. Businesses operating under both regulations must carefully navigate these differences to ensure compliance with both legal frameworks.

2. Definition of Personal Data in GDPR Vs CCPA

The **General Data Protection Regulation (GDPR)** and the **California Consumer Privacy Act (CCPA)** both define personal data broadly but emphasize different aspects. **GDPR** covers any information related to an **identified or identifiable person**, including **direct identifiers** (such as names and ID numbers) and **indirect identifiers** (like location data and online identifiers). It also categorizes certain types of sensitive data—such as **racial or ethnic origin, political opinions, religious beliefs, biometric data,**

and health information—as **"special categories"** that require stricter processing conditions. **CCPA**, on the other hand, defines **personal information** as any data that can be **linked to a consumer or household**, including **names, email addresses, IP addresses, purchasing history, and property records**. It places greater emphasis on **consumer transactions and commercial activities**, reflecting its focus on **consumer protection in business contexts**. While **GDPR provides a more detailed framework for protecting sensitive personal data**, **CCPA is designed to regulate consumer-related information, including household data and purchasing behaviors**.

3. Key Rights for Individuals here's a comparison of data subject rights under the General Data Protection Regulation (GDPR) and the California Consumer Privacy Act (CCPA)

The **General Data Protection Regulation (GDPR)** and the **California Consumer Privacy Act (CCPA)** both grant individual's rights over their personal data, but they differ in scope and focus. **GDPR** provides **comprehensive data rights**, including **access, portability, deletion, and rectification** of personal data. It also allows individuals to **restrict data processing** in certain cases and object to how their data is used. **CCPA**, on the other hand, focuses on **consumer empowerment**, giving California residents the right to **access, delete, and opt out of the sale of their personal information** but does not explicitly include **rectification or processing restrictions** like GDPR.

A key distinction is how they handle **data sales. GDPR allows individuals to object to data processing in general**, while **CCPA specifically grants consumers the right to opt out of data sales** to third parties. Both regulations emphasize **transparency**, requiring businesses to inform individuals about **what data is collected and how it is used**. However, **GDPR takes a broader approach**, covering **all personal data processing activities**, while **CCPA is more targeted**, focusing on consumer rights within **commercial transactions**. These differences highlight **GDPR's emphasis on fundamental privacy rights** versus **CCPA's goal of giving consumers control over their personal data in business interactions**.

4. Legal Basis for Data Processing

Under the General Data Protection Regulation (GDPR), organizations must establish a lawful basis before processing personal data. Article 6 of the GDPR outlines six legal bases: consent, contractual necessity, compliance with a legal obligation, protection of vital interests, performance of a task carried out in the public interest or in the exercise of official authority, and legitimate interests pursued by the data controller or a third party. Each basis has specific criteria and implications, and organizations are required to determine and document the appropriate basis for each processing activity. In contrast, the California

Consumer Privacy Act (CCPA) does not mandate that businesses establish a legal basis for processing personal information. Instead, the CCPA focuses on consumer rights, allowing individuals to opt out of the sale of their personal information and requiring businesses to provide transparency regarding data collection and sharing practices. This fundamental difference means that while the GDPR imposes proactive obligations on organizations to justify data processing activities, the CCPA emphasizes consumer control over personal information without prescribing specific lawful bases for processing.

5. Enforcement and Fines

The General Data Protection Regulation (GDPR) and the California Consumer Privacy Act (CCPA) have distinct enforcement mechanisms and penalties, differing in authority, scope, and financial impact. GDPR is enforced by supervisory authorities in each EU member state, which have broad investigative powers and can impose significant fines—up to €20 million or 4% of a company's global revenue, whichever is higher. Major tech firms have faced hefty penalties, such as Meta's €1.2 billion fine in 2023 and Uber's €290 million fine in 2024 for improper data transfers.

In contrast, CCPA enforcement falls under the California Attorney General and the California Privacy Protection Agency (CPPA). Penalties are lower than GDPR, with fines of up to $2,500 per unintentional violation and $7,500 for intentional violations or those involving minors' data. Additionally, consumers can sue businesses in cases of data breaches, with damages ranging from $100 to $750 per incident. Previously, businesses had 30 days to correct violations, but under the California Privacy Rights Act (CPRA), this grace period is now discretionary, allowing for quicker enforcement.

While both regulations seek to protect personal data, GDPR imposes stricter penalties and is enforced at a global scale, whereas CCPA applies only within California and provides consumers with more legal avenues to act. In summary, while both the GDPR and CCPA aim to protect personal data, the GDPR imposes more substantial fines and is enforced by dedicated data protection authorities across the EU. The CCPA, on the other hand, involves comparatively lower financial penalties and is enforced at the state level, with provisions for consumer-initiated lawsuits in specific circumstances. Businesses operating under both laws must carefully navigate compliance to avoid financial penalties and reputational damage.

6. Key Business Obligations

The General Data Protection Regulation (GDPR) and the California Consumer Privacy Act (CCPA) impose different obligations on businesses, reflecting their distinct approaches to data privacy. GDPR enforces comprehensive data protection standards globally, requiring organizations to maintain detailed records of data processing, especially for businesses with over 250 employees or those handling sensitive data. It also mandates the appointment of a Data Protection

Officer (DPO) in cases of large-scale data monitoring and requires businesses to report data breaches within 72 hours. However, GDPR does not specifically mandate opt-out mechanisms for data subjects.

In contrast, CCPA focuses on consumer control, particularly over the sale of personal data. It mandates that businesses provide opt-out options so consumers can prevent the sale of their information. While CCPA requires businesses to notify individuals of data breaches, it does not impose a strict reporting deadline like GDPR. Additionally, CCPA does not require businesses to appoint a DPO or maintain detailed processing records unless they engage in data sales.

While both laws reflect the global shift toward stronger privacy protections, GDPR is a broad, rights-based framework, while CCPA is more targeted, focusing on transparency and consumer choice. Businesses operating under both laws must carefully assess their compliance obligations based on how they process and handle personal data.

7. Geographic Focus

- **GDPR**: Protects EU residents globally.
- **CCPA**: Protects California residents only.

8. Consent Requirements

The General Data Protection Regulation (GDPR) and the California Consumer Privacy Act (CCPA) take different approaches to user consent and data processing. GDPR requires explicit, informed, and unambiguous opt-in consent before collecting personal data. Businesses must provide clear details on how the data will be used, who it will be shared with, and allow individuals to withdraw consent at any time. Failure to meet these strict consent requirements can lead to substantial penalties, emphasizing transparency and user control.

CCPA, on the other hand, primarily focuses on opt-out rights rather than requiring prior consent for data collection. Businesses must provide a "Do Not Sell My Personal Information" link, allowing consumers to opt out of the sale of their data. While general data processing does not require opt-in consent, stricter rules apply to minors—requiring explicit authorization for users under 16 and parental consent for those under 13.

These differences reflect GDPR's proactive approach, ensuring companies obtain permission before processing data, whereas CCPA's reactive model gives consumers the right to opt out of certain data-sharing practices. Businesses operating under both laws must carefully balance these consent mechanisms to remain compliant and uphold consumer privacy rights.

9. Consumer Rights in Practice

The General Data Protection Regulation (GDPR) and the California Consumer Privacy Act (CCPA) both grant individual's rights over their personal data, but they differ in scope and focus. GDPR provides broader individual rights, including data portability, allowing users to transfer their data between services, and rectification, which enables individuals to correct inaccurate information. It also grants the right to restrict data processing, meaning individuals can limit how their data is used under certain conditions, such as disputes over accuracy or legality.

In contrast, CCPA focuses on consumer control, particularly regarding data sales. One of its key provisions is the right to opt out, requiring businesses to provide a "Do Not Sell My Personal Information" link so consumers can prevent their data from being shared with third parties. It also includes the right to know, obligating businesses to disclose what personal data they collect, why they use it, and with whom they share it. Additionally, CCPA provides a limited private right of action, allowing consumers to sue businesses for data breaches resulting from poor security practices.

While GDPR offers more extensive personal data rights, including portability and processing restrictions, CCPA prioritizes transparency and consumer empowerment, particularly in commercial data practices. Understanding these differences is essential for both individuals seeking to protect their data and businesses ensuring compliance in these jurisdictions.

10. Transparency Obligations

Both the General Data Protection Regulation (GDPR) and the California Consumer Privacy Act (CCPA) emphasize transparency in data processing, but they differ in their requirements and focus. GDPR mandates detailed disclosures, requiring organizations to clearly inform individuals about why their data is collected, how it is used, who it is shared with, and how long it is retained. Privacy notices must be written in plain language and provided at the time of data collection to ensure individuals fully understand how their personal data is handled.

CCPA, on the other hand, focuses on consumer awareness, particularly regarding data sales. Businesses must disclose what types of personal data they collect, why they collect it, and which third parties they share or sell it to. A key requirement under CCPA is the "Do Not Sell My Personal Information" link, allowing consumers to easily opt out of data sales. Additionally, businesses must inform consumers of their rights to access, delete, and control their data and provide clear instructions on how to exercise these rights.

While GDPR takes a broad approach to transparency, covering all aspects of data processing, CCPA is more consumer-focused, emphasizing control over personal data sales. Businesses operating under both regulations must ensure their privacy policies and data handling practices align with the specific transparency obligations of each law to remain compliant.

11. Data Breach Notifications

Under the General Data Protection Regulation (GDPR), organizations are obligated to report personal data breaches to the relevant supervisory authority within 72 hours of becoming aware of the incident, unless the breach is unlikely to result in a risk to individuals' rights and freedoms. If the breach is likely to pose a high risk to affected individuals, the organization must also promptly inform those individuals. In contrast, the California Consumer Privacy Act (CCPA) requires businesses to notify consumers when their unencrypted personal information has been acquired, or is reasonably believed to have been acquired, by an unauthorized person. However, the CCPA does not specify a precise timeframe for such notifications. Notably, under the CCPA, consumers have the right to initiate legal action and seek damages if their personal information is compromised due to a business's failure to implement and maintain reasonable security procedures and practices.

12. Applicability to Businesses

The applicability of the General Data Protection Regulation (GDPR) and the California Consumer Privacy Act (CCPA) to businesses differs significantly in terms of scope, jurisdiction, and enforcement mechanisms. The GDPR applies broadly to any organization that processes the personal data of individuals residing in the European Union (EU), regardless of the organization's size or geographical location. This extraterritorial scope means that non-EU businesses must also comply if they offer goods or services to EU residents or monitor their online behavior, such as through cookies, analytics, or targeted advertising. In contrast, the CCPA has a narrower focus, applying only to for-profit businesses that meet specific criteria. A business falls under the CCPA's jurisdiction if it generates an annual gross revenue exceeding $25 million, collects or processes data from 100,000 or more California residents, or derives at least 50% of its revenue from selling consumers' personal information. Unlike the GDPR, which applies to any entity processing personal data, the CCPA does not cover non-profit organizations or government agencies.

13. Fines and Enforcement in Detail

The enforcement mechanisms and penalties for non-compliance also differ between the two regulations. The GDPR imposes higher penalties, with fines reaching up to €20 million or 4% of a company's total annual global revenue, whichever is higher. Enforcement is handled by supervisory authorities in each EU member state, which have the power to investigate organizations, issue warnings, and impose fines based on the severity of the violation. The GDPR adopts a tiered penalty structure, ensuring that more severe infractions, such as failure to obtain proper consent or unauthorized data transfers, receive heavier sanctions. On the other hand, the CCPA imposes significantly lower fines, with penalties set at $2,500 per violation and up to $7,500 for intentional violations. Enforcement falls primarily under the jurisdiction of the California Attorney General, though with the passage of the California Privacy Rights Act (CPRA), the California Privacy Protection Agency (CPPA) has also been granted authority to oversee compliance. Additionally, the CCPA allows consumers to file private lawsuits in specific cases, such as when a business fails to implement reasonable security measures, leading to a data breach that compromises personal information. This private right of action, absent in the GDPR, enables individuals to seek damages directly from businesses that fail to protect their data.

14. Impact on Businesses

The General Data Protection Regulation (GDPR) necessitates that businesses overhaul their systems and policies to achieve compliance. This includes appointing Data Protection Officers (DPOs), conducting Data Protection Impact Assessments (DPIAs), and implementing robust security measures such as encryption and pseudonymization. Conversely, the California Consumer Privacy Act (CCPA) primarily affects U.S. businesses, especially large organizations or data brokers. Its emphasis is less on internal business practices and more on ensuring consumers have control over their personal data.

15. Industry Implications

In the e-commerce sector, both the GDPR and the CCPA mandate that websites provide clear privacy notices and manage user data responsibly. The GDPR enforces stricter controls, requiring explicit consent for data processing, while the CCPA emphasizes transparency, particularly concerning the sale of personal data. For marketing practices, the GDPR restricts the use of personal data for targeted advertising unless explicit consent is obtained, thereby limiting unsolicited outreach. In contrast, the CCPA permits data tracking but obliges businesses to offer consumers opt-out options for data sales, granting individuals greater control over their information. Tech startups often encounter challenges in adhering to the GDPR's comprehensive requirements, which demand significant resources to ensure compliance. The CCPA, however, primarily affects larger entities, focusing on businesses with substantial revenues or extensive data handling, thus imposing fewer immediate burdens on smaller startups.

Global Influence

The General Data Protection Regulation (GDPR) and the California Consumer Privacy Act (CCPA) both aim to enhance data privacy, but they differ in their scope, focus, and enforcement. GDPR, implemented by the European Union in 2018, has set a global standard for data protection, influencing countries such as Canada, Brazil, and India to adopt similar privacy laws. In contrast, CCPA is a state-specific law that protects California residents, reflecting a growing trend of U.S. states developing their own privacy regulations, such as those in Colorado and Virginia.

A key difference between the two laws is their approach to consent. GDPR requires an opt-in model, meaning businesses must obtain explicit consent before collecting or processing personal data. CCPA, on the other hand, follows an opt-out model, allowing consumers to prevent the sale of their personal information but not requiring businesses to obtain prior approval for data collection. Additionally, GDPR applies to any business worldwide that processes the data of EU residents, while CCPA applies specifically to for-profit companies that meet certain criteria, such as annual revenue exceeding $25 million or handling data from 50,000 or more consumers.

When it comes to penalties, GDPR imposes strict fines of up to 4% of a company's global revenue, while CCPA penalties are capped at $7,500 per intentional violation. Enforcement also differs, with EU Supervisory Authorities overseeing GDPR compliance, while the California Attorney General enforces CCPA regulations.

Overall, GDPR is a comprehensive, global privacy framework that applies across industries and borders, whereas CCPA is a state-level consumer protection law focused on data transparency and control for Californians. Businesses operating under both laws must adopt a privacy-first approach, embedding data protection, security, and transparency into their operations to ensure compliance. As consumer awareness of data privacy grows, companies that proactively implement strong privacy practices will not only avoid legal risks but also build greater trust with their users in the digital economy.

Chapter 8: Comparison of GDPR and HIPAA

Comparison of GDPR and Health Privacy Laws in USA

The **General Data Protection Regulation (GDPR)** and the **Health Insurance Portability and Accountability Act (HIPAA)** are both designed to protect individuals' sensitive information, but they differ significantly in scope, purpose, and implementation. Here's a detailed comparison, specifically focusing on **health privacy**:

1. Scope of Application

The General Data Protection Regulation (GDPR) and the Health Insurance Portability and Accountability Act (HIPAA) are both pivotal in safeguarding health-related information, yet they differ markedly in their scope and applicability.

The GDPR, enacted by the European Union (EU), applies to all personal data of individuals within the EU, encompassing a wide array of information, including health data. This regulation is notable for its extraterritorial reach, meaning it governs any organization that processes the personal data of EU residents, irrespective of the organization's physical location or size. Consequently, even non-EU entities must comply with GDPR mandates if they offer goods or services to EU residents or monitor their behavior online. Within the GDPR framework, health data is classified as a "special category" of personal data, which entails stricter processing conditions due to its sensitive nature. Organizations handling such data must adhere to enhanced protective measures to ensure compliance.

In contrast, HIPAA is a United States federal law specifically designed to protect "protected health information" (PHI) within the U.S. healthcare system. Its provisions are primarily directed at "covered entities," which include healthcare providers, health plans, and healthcare clearinghouses, as well as their "business associates"—third-party vendors that handle PHI on behalf of these entities. HIPAA's jurisdiction is confined to the healthcare sector, focusing exclusively on entities that deal directly with PHI. Unlike the GDPR's broad applicability, HIPAA does not extend its reach to organizations outside the U.S. healthcare domain, nor does it cover all forms of personal data, concentrating solely on health-related information.

Understanding these distinctions is crucial for organizations operating across both jurisdictions. While the GDPR imposes comprehensive obligations on any entity processing EU residents' personal data, including health information, HIPAA's requirements are more narrowly tailored to specific players within the U.S. healthcare industry. Compliance strategies must, therefore, be adapted to meet the specific demands of each regulatory framework, ensuring that health data is protected in accordance with the pertinent legal standards.

2. Definition of Health Data

The General Data Protection Regulation (GDPR) and the Health Insurance Portability and Accountability Act (HIPAA) both address the protection of health-related information, but they differ significantly in their definitions and scopes.

Under the GDPR, "data concerning health" is defined as personal data related to the physical or mental health of an individual, encompassing information about the past, present, or future health status. This includes data collected during the provision of health care services, which reveal information about an individual's health status. The GDPR's broad definition covers a wide range of data, such as medical histories, genetic and biometric data, and information gathered by health and wellness applications or wearable devices. Any data that can identify an individual and pertains to their health is afforded protection under the GDPR. Notably, health data is categorized as a special category of personal data under the GDPR, subjecting it to stricter processing conditions due to its sensitive nature.

In contrast, HIPAA specifically protects "protected health information" (PHI) within the United States. PHI refers to individually identifiable health information that is created, received, stored, or transmitted by covered entities, which include health care providers, health plans, and health care clearinghouses, as well as their business associates. This encompasses a variety of data, such as names, addresses, medical records, insurance details, and other information linked to health services. However, HIPAA's protections are limited to data handled by these covered entities and do not extend to health information collected by entities outside the traditional health care system. For instance, data gathered by fitness applications or wearable devices not managed by covered entities fall outside HIPAA's jurisdiction.

Understanding these distinctions is crucial for organizations operating across different jurisdictions, as the scope of protected health information varies between the GDPR and HIPAA. While the GDPR offers a comprehensive framework protecting a wide array of health-related data, HIPAA's focus is narrower, concentrating on information managed within the U.S. health care system by specific entities.

3. Consent and Legal Basis for Data Use

The General Data Protection Regulation (GDPR) and the Health Insurance Portability and Accountability Act (HIPAA) establish distinct frameworks governing the use and disclosure of health-related data, each with specific stipulations regarding consent and legal bases for processing such information.

Under the GDPR, processing health data necessitates a valid legal basis, especially given its classification as "special category data," which warrants enhanced protection due to its sensitive nature. Several legal grounds permit the processing of health data: obtaining explicit consent from the individual; fulfilling legal obligations; protecting vital interests, particularly in life-threatening situations; and serving public health purposes. When relying on consent, it must be explicit, informed, and specific, ensuring that individuals are fully aware of how their data will be utilized. Organizations are obligated to provide clear and comprehensive notices detailing the purposes of data collection, processing methods, and any potential data sharing with third parties. This transparency is fundamental to upholding individuals' rights and fostering trust in data handling practices.

In contrast, HIPAA, which governs protected health information (PHI) within the United States, does not always require explicit patient consent for the use or disclosure of PHI. The regulation permits covered entities—such as healthcare providers, health plans, and healthcare clearinghouses—to use or disclose PHI without patient authorization for purposes directly related to treatment, payment, and healthcare operations. This allowance facilitates essential healthcare functions by enabling the seamless sharing of information necessary for patient care and administrative processes. However, for uses and disclosures beyond these core functions, such as marketing activities or certain types of research, HIPAA mandates obtaining explicit patient authorization. This authorization must be detailed and specific, clearly outlining the intended use or disclosure, ensuring that patients retain control over how their sensitive health information is utilized in contexts that extend beyond standard healthcare operations.

Understanding these regulatory nuances is crucial for organizations operating within or across jurisdictions governed by GDPR and HIPAA. While the GDPR emphasizes obtaining explicit consent and providing detailed information about data processing activities, HIPAA focuses on facilitating healthcare delivery and related operations, requiring patient authorization primarily for non-routine uses of PHI. Compliance with these regulations necessitates tailored approaches that respect the specific legal requirements and underlying principles of each framework, thereby ensuring the protection of individuals' health information and maintaining organizational accountability.

4. Data Subject Rights

The General Data Protection Regulation (GDPR) and the Health Insurance Portability and Accountability Act (HIPAA) both establish frameworks to protect individuals' data, yet they differ significantly in the rights they grant concerning personal and health information.

Access to Personal Data

Under the GDPR, individuals, referred to as data subjects, have the unequivocal right to access their personal data held by organizations. This means they can request confirmation on whether their data is being processed and, if so, obtain a copy of that data along with supplementary information about the processing activities. Similarly, HIPAA grants patients the right to access their Protected Health Information (PHI) maintained by covered entities, such as healthcare providers and health plans. Patients can inspect and obtain a copy of their medical records, ensuring transparency in their healthcare information.

Data Correction

Both regulations recognize the individual's right to rectify inaccuracies. The GDPR provides data subjects with the right to have incorrect or incomplete personal data corrected without undue delay. HIPAA mirrors this by allowing patients to request amendments to their PHI if they believe it is incorrect or incomplete. Covered entities are generally required to act on such requests, ensuring the accuracy of health records.

Data Portability

A distinctive feature of the GDPR is the right to data portability. This empowers individuals to receive their personal data in a structured, commonly used, and machine-readable format and to transmit that data to another controller without hindrance. This facilitates seamless data transfer between service providers. In contrast, HIPAA does not encompass a right to data portability; its provisions focus on access and amendment rights without obligating entities to provide data in a transferable format.

Right to Erasure (Deletion)

The GDPR introduces the "right to be forgotten," allowing individuals to request the deletion of their personal data under specific circumstances, such as when the data is no longer necessary for the purposes it was collected or if the individual withdraws consent. However, this right is not absolute and is subject to certain exceptions. Conversely, HIPAA does not grant patients the right to have their medical records deleted. Healthcare providers are often required to retain medical records for specific periods, as dictated by state laws or institutional policies, to ensure continuity of care and for legal compliance.

Restriction on Processing

Under the GDPR, individuals have the right to restrict the processing of their personal data under certain conditions, such as when they contest the accuracy of the data or object to its processing. During such restrictions, organizations are generally prohibited from processing the data, aside from storing it. HIPAA does not explicitly provide a right to restrict the processing of PHI. While patients can request restrictions on the use or disclosure of their health information, covered entities are not obligated to agree to such requests, except in specific situations like when the disclosure is to a health plan for payment or healthcare operations and the patient has paid out-of-pocket in full for the service.

Notification of Data Breach

Both regulations mandate that individuals be informed in the event of a data breach involving their information. The GDPR requires data controllers to notify the appropriate supervisory authority within 72 hours of becoming aware of a personal data breach. If the breach poses a high risk to individuals' rights and freedoms, the affected individuals must also be informed without undue delay. HIPAA mandates that covered entities notify affected individuals without unreasonable delay and no later than 60 days following the discovery of a breach of unsecured PHI. This notification must include a description of the breach, the types of information involved, steps individuals should take to protect themselves, and measures the entity is taking to investigate and mitigate the breach.

In summary, while both the GDPR and HIPAA aim to protect individuals' information, the rights afforded under each differ in scope and application. The GDPR offers a broader range of rights concerning personal data across various sectors, emphasizing individual control over data. HIPAA, focused on the healthcare sector within the United States, provides specific rights pertaining to the access and amendment of health information, with less emphasis on data portability and deletion.

5. Security Requirements

The General Data Protection Regulation (GDPR) and the Health Insurance Portability and Accountability

Act (HIPAA) both establish stringent security requirements to protect sensitive information, yet they approach these obligations differently, reflecting their distinct scopes and objectives.

GDPR Security Requirements

Under the GDPR, organizations are mandated to implement appropriate technical and organizational measures to ensure a level of security commensurate with the risk associated with personal data processing. This risk-based approach requires entities to consider factors such as the state of the art, implementation costs, and the nature, scope, context, and purposes of processing. Key measures include:

- **Encryption and Pseudonymization:** Protecting personal data by rendering it unintelligible to unauthorized individuals.
- **Confidentiality, Integrity, Availability, and Resilience:** Ensuring that processing systems and services are secure and reliable.
- **Restoration Capabilities:** Ability to restore personal data access and availability promptly after a physical or technical incident.
- **Regular Testing and Evaluation:** Ongoing assessment of the effectiveness of security measures to adapt to evolving risks.

Additionally, for processing activities likely to result in high risks to individuals' rights and freedoms, organizations must conduct Data Protection Impact

Assessments (DPIAs) to identify and mitigate potential hazards. Accountability is a cornerstone of the GDPR, obligating organizations to not only implement these measures but also to document and demonstrate compliance actively.

HIPAA Security Requirements

HIPAA focuses on safeguarding electronic Protected Health Information (ePHI) within the U.S. healthcare system. The HIPAA Security Rule delineates specific safeguards across three primary categories:

- **Administrative Safeguards:** Policies and procedures designed to manage the selection, development, and implementation of security measures. This includes conducting regular risk analyses to identify potential vulnerabilities, implementing workforce training programs, and establishing contingency plans for emergencies.
- **Physical Safeguards:** Measures to protect electronic information systems and related buildings and equipment from natural and environmental hazards, as well as unauthorized intrusion. Examples include controlled facility access, secure workstation locations, and device and media controls to manage hardware and electronic media.
- **Technical Safeguards:** The technology and related policies that protect ePHI and control access to it. This encompasses access controls

like unique user identifications, encryption mechanisms to protect data during transmission, and audit controls to record and examine activity in information systems.

A fundamental aspect of HIPAA's approach is the "minimum necessary" standard, which dictates that ePHI should only be accessed or disclosed to the extent needed to fulfill a specific purpose. Regular risk assessments are imperative, enabling organizations to identify potential threats and implement appropriate measures to mitigate them.

Comparative Insights

While both GDPR and HIPAA emphasize the protection of sensitive information through robust security measures, their scopes differ. The GDPR applies broadly to all personal data processing activities involving EU residents, imposing a comprehensive framework for data protection across various sectors. In contrast, HIPAA specifically targets the healthcare industry within the United States, focusing on the protection of health information handled by covered entities and their business associates.

Organizations subject to both regulations must navigate these requirements carefully, ensuring that their security measures align with the stringent standards set forth by each. This necessitates a thorough understanding of the specific obligations under each framework and the implementation of tailored strategies to achieve compliance, thereby safeguarding sensitive data effectively across different regulatory landscapes.

6. Breach Notification

The General Data Protection Regulation (GDPR) and the Health Insurance Portability and Accountability Act (HIPAA) both establish stringent protocols for breach notification, yet they differ in scope, timelines, and specific requirements.

GDPR Breach Notification Requirements

Under the GDPR, organizations acting as data controllers are obligated to report personal data breaches to the relevant supervisory authority without undue delay and, where feasible, within 72 hours of becoming aware of the breach. This prompt notification is mandatory unless the breach is unlikely to result in a risk to the rights and freedoms of natural persons. If the notification is not made within the 72-hour window, the organization must provide reasons for the delay. Furthermore, if the breach is likely to result in a high risk to the affected individuals, the organization must also communicate the breach to the data subjects without undue delay, ensuring they are informed about the nature of the breach, potential consequences, and measures taken or proposed to mitigate its adverse effects.

HIPAA Breach Notification Requirements

In contrast, HIPAA outlines specific breach notification obligations for covered entities and their business associates concerning unsecured protected health information (PHI). Upon discovering a breach, covered entities must notify the affected individuals without unreasonable delay and no later than 60 days following the discovery of the breach. The notification should include a description of the breach, the types of information involved, steps individuals should take to protect themselves, and measures the entity is taking to investigate and mitigate the breach. Additionally, if the breach affects 500 or more individuals, the covered entity is required to notify the Secretary of the Department of Health and Human Services (HHS) contemporaneously with the individual notices. In cases where the breach impacts more than 500 residents of a state or jurisdiction, prominent media outlets serving the affected area must also be informed. For breaches affecting fewer than 500 individuals, the covered entity may notify the Secretary of HHS on an annual basis.

Comparative Analysis

The GDPR mandates a more accelerated notification timeline, requiring reports to supervisory authorities within 72 hours, reflecting its emphasis on rapid response to potential risks to individual rights and freedoms. HIPAA, while also prioritizing timely notification, allows up to 60 days for informing affected individuals and the HHS, acknowledging the complexities involved in thoroughly investigating breaches within the healthcare sector. Moreover, HIPAA's requirements are specifically tailored to breaches involving PHI within the U.S. healthcare system, whereas the GDPR encompasses a broader spectrum of personal data breaches across various sectors and jurisdictions involving EU residents.

Understanding these distinctions is crucial for organizations operating under both regulatory frameworks, as compliance necessitates adherence to the specific breach notification protocols outlined by each.

7. Enforcement and Penalties

The General Data Protection Regulation (GDPR) and the Health Insurance Portability and Accountability Act (HIPAA) establish distinct enforcement mechanisms and penalty structures to ensure compliance with their respective data protection mandates.

GDPR Enforcement and Penalties

Under the GDPR, supervisory authorities in each European Union (EU) member state, known as Data Protection Authorities (DPAs), are responsible for monitoring and enforcing compliance. These authorities possess investigative and corrective powers, including the ability to impose administrative fines on organizations that violate GDPR provisions. The regulation delineates two tiers of maximum penalties: for severe infringements, fines can reach up to €20 million or 4% of the organization's total worldwide annual turnover of the preceding financial year, whichever is higher; for less severe violations, the fines can be up to €10 million or 2% of the global annual turnover. The determination of fine amounts considers various factors, such as the nature, gravity, and duration of the infringement, as well as any measures taken by the organization to mitigate the damage. Notably, enforcement actions have led to substantial fines; for instance, in 2023, Meta Platforms was fined over €1.2 billion for data transfer violations, underscoring the rigorous application of GDPR penalties.

HIPAA Enforcement and Penalties

In the United States, HIPAA enforcement is primarily managed by the Office for Civil Rights (OCR) within the Department of Health and Human Services (HHS). The OCR investigates complaints, conducts compliance reviews, and can impose civil monetary penalties on covered entities and business associates that fail to adhere to HIPAA requirements. HIPAA outlines a tiered penalty structure based on the level of culpability associated with the violation:

- **Tier 1:** Violations where the entity was unaware and could not have reasonably avoided the violation, even with reasonable diligence. Penalties range from \$100 to \$50,000 per violation, with an annual maximum of \$25,000 for repeat violations.
- **Tier 2:** Violations due to reasonable cause, not involving willful neglect. Penalties range from \$1,000 to \$50,000 per violation, with an annual maximum of \$100,000 for repeat violations.

- **Tier 3:** Violations resulting from willful neglect that are corrected within a required time. Penalties range from $10,000 to $50,000 per violation, with an annual maximum of $250,000 for repeat violations.
- **Tier 4:** Violations resulting from willful neglect that are not corrected. Penalties are $50,000 per violation, with an annual maximum of $1.5 million.

These penalties are subject to annual adjustments for inflation. In addition to civil penalties, certain violations may lead to criminal charges, especially in cases involving deliberate misuse of protected health information (PHI). Enforcement actions have resulted in significant financial penalties; as of December 2024, the OCR has settled or imposed civil money penalties in 152 cases, totaling approximately $144.88 million.

Comparative Analysis

While both GDPR and HIPAA aim to protect sensitive information, their enforcement frameworks and penalty structures reflect differences in scope and jurisdiction. The GDPR applies broadly to all organizations processing personal data of EU residents, regardless of the organization's location, and imposes potentially higher fines based on global revenue, emphasizing the protection of personal data across various sectors. In contrast, HIPAA specifically targets entities within the U.S. healthcare system, with penalties scaled according to the nature of the violation and the entity's level of culpability. Organizations operating under these regulations must understand and comply with the respective requirements to avoid substantial penalties and ensure the protection of individuals' data rights.

8. Global and Industry Influence

The General Data Protection Regulation (GDPR) has significantly influenced global data privacy standards, inspiring countries like Brazil and India to enact similar comprehensive data protection laws. Brazil's Lei Geral de Proteção de Dados (LGPD), effective since September 2020, mirrors the GDPR in its core principles, emphasizing transparency, data minimization, and granting individuals rights over their personal data. The LGPD applies to any organization processing data of Brazilian citizens, regardless of the organization's location, thereby extending its reach beyond national borders.

Similarly, India's proposed data protection legislation reflects GDPR's influence, aiming to establish robust privacy frameworks that align with global standards. The GDPR's extraterritorial applicability and stringent requirements have prompted organizations worldwide to reassess their data handling practices to ensure compliance, thereby setting a global benchmark for data protection.

In contrast, the Health Insurance Portability and Accountability Act (HIPAA) primarily impacts healthcare privacy practices within the United States. HIPAA establishes national standards for protecting sensitive patient information, focusing on entities such as healthcare providers, health plans, and healthcare clearinghouses. However, its scope is limited to these covered entities and their business associates, excluding many consumer-facing health applications and devices. For instance, fitness trackers and wellness apps that collect health-related data but are not offered by covered entities fall outside HIPAA's jurisdiction. This regulatory gap has raised concerns, as users often mistakenly believe that all health-related data is protected under HIPAA, leaving data collected by these apps potentially vulnerable to unauthorized sharing or misuse.

Consequently, while HIPAA plays a crucial role in safeguarding medical information within the traditional healthcare system, it does not extend its protections to the broader ecosystem of health-related technologies and services.

The differing scopes of GDPR and HIPAA highlight the challenges in creating uniform data protection standards across various industries and jurisdictions. While GDPR's comprehensive approach influences global data privacy reforms across multiple sectors, HIPAA's specialized focus underscores the need for updated regulations that address emerging technologies and the evolving landscape of health data collection and usage.

9. Key Similarities

The General Data Protection Regulation (GDPR) and the Health Insurance Portability and Accountability

Act (HIPAA) are both pivotal regulations designed to safeguard sensitive information, and they share several key similarities in their approaches to data protection.

Robust Security Measures

Both GDPR and HIPAA mandate the implementation of stringent security protocols to protect sensitive data from unauthorized access, breaches, and other cyber threats. Under the GDPR, organizations are required to adopt appropriate technical and organizational measures, such as encryption and pseudonymization, to ensure a level of security commensurate with the risk associated with personal data processing. Similarly, HIPAA's Security Rule obligates covered entities and their business associates to implement administrative, physical, and technical safeguards. These include access controls, audit controls, integrity controls, and transmission security measures to protect electronic Protected Health Information (ePHI) from unauthorized access or alterations. Both regulations emphasize the necessity of regular risk assessments and the continuous monitoring and updating of security practices to adapt to evolving threats.

Individual Access and Control Over Data

Empowering individuals with rights over their personal information is a cornerstone of both GDPR and HIPAA. The GDPR grants data subjects comprehensive rights, including the right to access their personal data, rectify inaccuracies, and, in certain circumstances, request the erasure of their data. Organizations are obligated to respond to such requests promptly, typically within one month. HIPAA also provides patients with rights concerning their health information. Patients have the right to access and obtain copies of their medical records and request amendments if they identify inaccuracies. While HIPAA does not encompass a right to erasure akin to the GDPR, it ensures that patients can exercise significant control over their health information, including obtaining an accounting of disclosures made by the covered entity.

Breach Notification Requirements

Both regulations establish clear protocols for notifying individuals and authorities in the event of a data breach involving protected information. The GDPR mandates that data controllers report personal data breaches to the relevant supervisory authority without undue delay and, where feasible, within 72 hours of becoming aware of the breach. If the breach is likely to result in a high risk to the rights and freedoms of individuals, the affected data subjects must also be informed promptly. HIPAA's Breach Notification Rule requires covered entities to notify affected individuals following the discovery of a breach of unsecured Protected Health Information (PHI). Notifications must be provided without unreasonable delay and no later than 60 days from the discovery of the breach. For breaches affecting 500 or more individuals, entities must also notify the Department of Health and Human Services (HHS) and, in certain cases, prominent media outlets. These notification requirements in both GDPR and HIPAA aim to ensure transparency and allow individuals to take necessary actions to protect themselves from potential harm resulting from data breaches.

In summary, while the GDPR and HIPAA operate within different jurisdictions and scopes—the GDPR having a broad applicability across various sectors and the HIPAA focusing specifically on the U.S. healthcare industry—they converge on fundamental principles. Both emphasize the importance of robust security measures, grant individuals' significant rights over their data, and require prompt notification in the event of data breaches, reflecting a shared commitment to protecting sensitive information in an increasingly digital landscape.

10. Key Differences

The General Data Protection Regulation (GDPR) and the Health Insurance Portability and Accountability Act (HIPAA) are both pivotal in safeguarding sensitive information, yet they differ significantly across several key aspects, including geographic scope, data protection focus, consent requirements, rights to data deletion, and enforcement mechanisms.

Geographic Scope

The GDPR is a comprehensive data protection regulation that applies to all organizations, irrespective of their location, that process the personal data of individuals residing within the European Union

(EU). This extraterritorial applicability ensures that EU residents' data is protected globally, compelling international organizations to comply with its stringent standards when handling EU citizens' information. In contrast, HIPAA is a United States federal law specifically designed to regulate the use and disclosure of Protected Health Information (PHI) within the U.S. healthcare sector. Its jurisdiction is confined to covered entities and their business associates operating within the United States, focusing on the domestic management of health-related data.

Type of Data Protected

GDPR encompasses a broad spectrum of personal data, including health-related information, without restriction to any industry. It defines personal data as any information relating to an identified or identifiable natural person, thereby covering a wide array of data types across various sectors. HIPAA, however, specifically targets PHI, which pertains to individually identifiable health information maintained or transmitted by covered entities and their business associates. This includes medical records, billing information, and any data related to an individual's physical or mental health condition, treatment, or payment for healthcare services.

Consent Requirements

Under the GDPR, obtaining explicit consent from individuals is a fundamental prerequisite for processing personal data, especially when it involves sensitive categories such as health information. This consent must be freely given, specific, informed, and unambiguous, ensuring that individuals are fully aware of how their data will be used and have actively agreed to such processing. HIPAA's approach to consent differs; it permits the use and disclosure of PHI without patient authorization for purposes directly related to treatment, payment, and healthcare operations. For uses beyond these core functions, such as marketing or research activities, HIPAA requires covered entities to obtain explicit patient authorization, thereby delineating between routine healthcare activities and other purposes.

Right to Deletion

The GDPR grants individuals the "right to be forgotten," allowing them to request the erasure of their personal data under specific circumstances, such as when the data is no longer necessary for the purposes for which it was collected or if the individual withdraws consent. This empowers individuals to have greater control over their personal information and its retention. Conversely, HIPAA does not provide a similar right to deletion. While patients can request amendments to their medical records to correct inaccuracies, healthcare providers are generally required to retain PHI for a specified period, often mandated by state laws or institutional policies, to ensure continuity of care and compliance with legal obligations.

Enforcement Mechanisms

Enforcement of the GDPR is carried out by Data Protection Authorities (DPAs) in each EU member state. These authorities are empowered to investigate violations, impose administrative fines, and ensure organizations adhere to data protection principles. The penalties for non-compliance can be substantial, reaching up to €20 million or 4% of the organization's total worldwide annual turnover, whichever is higher. HIPAA enforcement, on the other hand, is overseen by the Office for Civil Rights (OCR) within the U.S. Department of Health and Human Services (HHS). The OCR is responsible for investigating complaints, conducting compliance reviews, and imposing civil monetary penalties for violations. HIPAA's penalty structure is tiered based on the nature and extent of the violation, with fines ranging from $100 to $50,000 per violation, capped at $1.5 million per year for identical provisions.

Understanding these distinctions is crucial for organizations operating across both jurisdictions, as compliance requires navigating the specific requirements and obligations set forth by each regulation to effectively protect individuals' sensitive information.

Conclusion

The General Data Protection Regulation (GDPR) and the Health Insurance Portability and Accountability Act (HIPAA) are both pivotal in safeguarding health-related data, yet they differ significantly in scope, applicability, and regulatory focus. The GDPR adopts a comprehensive, global approach, aiming to protect all personal data, including health information, of individuals within the European Union (EU). It enforces stringent rules regarding consent, individual rights, and data security, thereby influencing privacy laws worldwide. For instance, Brazil's Lei Geral de Proteção de Dados (LGPD) mirrors the GDPR's principles, extending similar protections to Brazilian citizens. In contrast, HIPAA is a U.S.-specific regulation focusing exclusively on the healthcare sector. It ensures the confidentiality and security of Protected Health Information (PHI) within U.S. healthcare operations, primarily affecting healthcare providers, health plans, and their business associates.

For organizations operating internationally or within overlapping sectors such as telehealth and health applications, navigating the regulatory landscapes of both GDPR and HIPAA is imperative to mitigate legal risks. Telehealth platforms, for example, must ensure compliance with HIPAA by implementing secure communication channels, access controls, and data encryption to protect PHI during electronic transmission. Simultaneously, if these platforms serve EU residents, they must adhere to GDPR mandates, which may include obtaining explicit consent for processing health data and ensuring data subjects can exercise their rights, such as accessing or deleting their information. The dual compliance requirement necessitates a robust data protection framework that aligns with both regulations, addressing aspects like data storage, user consent, and breach notification protocols.

The practical implications for organizations are multifaceted. Achieving compliance involves conducting thorough data mapping to understand data flows across jurisdictions, implementing comprehensive privacy policies that meet both GDPR and HIPAA standards, and investing in technological solutions that offer the necessary security measures. Challenges include reconciling differences between the regulations, such as the GDPR's broader definition of personal data versus HIPAA's specific focus on PHI and managing cross-border data transfers in a manner compliant with GDPR's stringent requirements. Strategies for effective compliance encompass regular staff training on data protection practices, appointing dedicated privacy officers to oversee compliance efforts, and engaging in continuous monitoring and auditing to identify and rectify potential vulnerabilities. By proactively addressing these challenges, organizations can build trust with users, avoid substantial penalties, and ensure the responsible handling of sensitive health information across diverse regulatory environments.

Part 4: Gaps in Privacy Protection in the US

Gaps in Privacy Protection in the US

The current US privacy framework has several notable gaps, primarily due to the absence of a comprehensive federal privacy law. Unlike the European Union's GDPR, the US relies on a patchwork of state laws and sector-specific regulations, such as the California Consumer Privacy Act (CCPA), the Health Insurance Portability and Accountability Act (HIPAA), and the Children's Online Privacy Protection Act (COPPA). This fragmented approach leads to inconsistencies in privacy protections across different states and industries, creating challenges for both consumers and businesses.

One significant gap is the lack of uniformity in privacy rights and protections. For instance, while the CCPA grants California residents specific rights over their personal data, such as the right to access, delete, and opt-out of the sale of their information, these rights are not universally available to all US citizens. This disparity can lead to confusion and unequal protection for individuals depending on their location.

Additionally, the rapid advancement of new technologies poses further challenges to privacy protection. Emerging technologies like artificial intelligence (AI), the Internet of Things (IoT), and blockchain often require the collection and processing of vast amounts of personal data. These technologies can outpace existing privacy regulations, leading to vulnerabilities and potential misuse of data. For example, AI systems can inadvertently perpetuate biases or make decisions based on sensitive personal information, raising ethical and privacy concerns.

Moreover, the hyperconnectivity of modern devices increases the risk of data breaches and cyberattacks. As more devices become interconnected, a vulnerability in one system can have cascading effects, compromising the privacy and security of vast amounts of data. This interconnectedness necessitates robust and adaptive privacy protections that can keep pace with technological advancements.

The lack of a comprehensive federal privacy law and the challenges posed by new technologies highlight significant gaps in the US privacy framework. Addressing these gaps is crucial to ensuring consistent and effective privacy protections for all US citizens.

Chapter 9:

Implications of Privacy Gaps and Handling of Children's Data

The gaps in the US privacy framework have several significant implications for both individuals and businesses:

For Individuals

1. **Inconsistent Privacy Protections**: The lack of a comprehensive federal privacy law means that privacy protections vary widely depending on the state and sector. This inconsistency can lead to confusion among consumers about their rights and the level of protection they can expect.

2. **Increased Risk of Data Breaches**: Without uniform standards, companies may not implement robust data protection measures, increasing the risk of data breaches. These breaches can expose sensitive personal information, leading to identity theft, financial loss, and other harms.

3. **Limited Control Over Personal Data**: Many US citizens have limited control over how their personal data is collected, used, and shared. Unlike GDPR, which grants individuals specific rights over their data, US laws often lack such comprehensive provisions.

For Businesses

1. **Compliance Challenges**: Businesses operating across multiple states face the challenge of navigating a complex web of state-specific privacy laws. This can lead to increased compliance costs and legal uncertainties.

2. **Reputational Risks**: Companies that fail to adequately protect consumer data or comply with varying privacy regulations risk damaging their reputation. This can result in loss of consumer trust and potential financial penalties.

3. **Competitive Disadvantage**: US companies may find themselves at a competitive disadvantage compared to their counterparts in regions with stricter privacy regulations, such as the EU. Consumers increasingly value privacy and may prefer to do business with companies that offer stronger data protection.

Broader Implications

1. **Economic Impact**: The economic impact of data breaches and cybercrime is substantial. Cybercrime costs are projected to rise significantly, affecting both businesses and consumers.

2. **Public Trust**: The lack of comprehensive privacy protections can erode public trust in digital services and technologies. This mistrust can

hinder the adoption of new technologies and limit the potential benefits they offer.

3. **Global Standing**: The US may lag behind other countries in establishing a robust privacy framework, potentially affecting its global standing in data protection and digital innovation.

Addressing these gaps through comprehensive federal privacy legislation could help mitigate these implications, providing consistent protections for individuals and a clearer regulatory environment for businesses.

Economic Impact of Privacy Protection Gaps in the US

The gaps in the US privacy framework have significant economic implications, affecting both businesses and consumers. Here are some key aspects to consider:

Costs of Data Breaches

Data breaches can have substantial financial consequences. The FBI and IMF estimate that cybercrime cost the world $8.4 trillion (about $26,000 per person in the US) in 2022 and could rise to over $25 trillion (about $77,000 per person in the US) by 2027. In the US, the lack of comprehensive privacy protections increases the risk of data breaches, leading to direct costs such as legal fees, fines, and compensation to affected individuals. Indirect costs include reputational damage and loss of consumer trust, which can have long-term impacts on business revenue.

Compliance Costs

Businesses operating in the US face high compliance costs due to the fragmented privacy regulations. Navigating a complex web of state-specific laws requires significant investment in legal expertise and compliance infrastructure. These costs can be particularly burdensome for small and medium-sized enterprises (SMEs), which may lack the resources to effectively manage compliance across multiple jurisdictions.

Impact on Innovation

The absence of a unified privacy framework can stifle innovation. Companies may be hesitant to invest in new technologies or data-driven solutions due to uncertainties around compliance and potential legal risks. For example, the proposed American Privacy Rights Act's data minimization policy could inhibit companies' ability to innovate with data, deliver efficient services, and grow the economy. This uncertainty can lead to a chilling effect on innovation, as businesses may avoid collecting and using data that could drive technological advancements.

Economic Inefficiencies

The fragmented privacy landscape creates economic inefficiencies. Businesses must duplicate efforts to comply with varying state laws, leading to redundant processes and increased operational costs. These inefficiencies can reduce overall productivity and competitiveness, impacting the broader economy.

Consumer Trust and Market Dynamics

Strong privacy protections are essential for building consumer trust. When consumers feel their data is secure, they are more likely to engage with digital services and technologies. Conversely, gaps in privacy protection can erode trust, leading to reduced adoption of new technologies and services. This can limit market growth and the potential benefits of digital innovation.

Global Competitiveness

The US may lag other countries in establishing robust privacy protections, affecting its global competitiveness. Regions with stricter privacy regulations, like the EU, may attract more investment and innovation in data-driven industries. This can lead to a competitive disadvantage for US companies, as consumers and businesses increasingly prioritize privacy and data security.

The economic impact of privacy protection gaps in the US is multifaceted, affecting costs, innovation, efficiency, consumer trust, and global competitiveness. Addressing these gaps through comprehensive federal privacy legislation could help mitigate these economic challenges and foster a more secure and innovative digital economy.

Consumer Trust and Privacy Protection

Consumer trust is a critical component of the digital economy, and privacy protection plays a significant role in building and maintaining this trust. Here are some key aspects to consider:

Impact of Data Privacy Concerns on Consumer Trust

1. **Transparency and Control**: Consumers are more likely to trust companies that are transparent about their data practices and provide them with control over their personal information. When companies clearly communicate how data is collected, used, and shared, and offer easy-to-use tools for managing privacy preferences, it fosters trust.

2. **Data Breaches and Trust Erosion**: Data breaches can severely damage consumer trust. When personal information is exposed due to a breach, consumers may feel vulnerable and lose confidence in the company's ability to protect their data. This can lead to a decline in customer loyalty and a negative impact on the company's reputation.

3. **Privacy Policies and Practices**: The presence of robust privacy policies and practices can enhance consumer trust. Companies that adhere to high standards of data protection and comply with privacy regulations demonstrate their commitment to safeguarding consumer data, which can positively influence trust.

Factors Influencing Consumer Trust

1. **Perceived Security**: Consumers need to feel that their data is secure. Implementing strong

security measures, such as encryption and regular security audits, can reassure consumers that their information is protected.

2. **Regulatory Compliance**: Compliance with privacy regulations, such as GDPR or CCPA, can enhance consumer trust. These regulations set high standards for data protection and give consumers rights over their personal data, which can increase their confidence in how their data is handled.

3. **Responsiveness to Privacy Concerns**: Companies that are responsive to privacy concerns and take proactive steps to address them can build stronger trust with consumers. This includes promptly notifying consumers of data breaches and taking corrective actions to prevent future incidents.

Economic Implications of Consumer Trust

1. **Customer Loyalty and Retention**: Trust is a key driver of customer loyalty. Consumers who trust a company are more likely to continue using its services and recommend it to others. This can lead to increased customer retention and a positive impact on the company's bottom line.

2. **Competitive Advantage**: Companies that prioritize privacy protection can gain a competitive advantage. As consumers become more aware of privacy issues, they are more likely to choose businesses that demonstrate a strong commitment to protecting their data.

3. **Market Growth**: Trust in digital services and technologies is essential for market growth. When consumers trust that their data is safe, they are more likely to adopt new technologies and engage with digital platforms, driving innovation and economic growth.

In summary, consumer trust is deeply intertwined with privacy protection. Companies that prioritize transparency, security, and regulatory compliance can build and maintain trust, leading to increased customer loyalty, a competitive edge, and overall market growth.

The Role of Social Media in Consumer Trust

Social media plays a pivotal role in shaping consumer trust, influencing how individuals perceive brands and make purchasing decisions. Here are some key aspects to consider:

Transparency and Authenticity

1. **Direct Communication**: Social media platforms allow brands to communicate directly with consumers, fostering transparency and authenticity. By sharing behind-the-scenes content, responding to customer inquiries, and addressing concerns publicly, brands can build trust and demonstrate their commitment to customer satisfaction.

2. **User-Generated Content**: Encouraging user-generated content, such as reviews, testimonials, and social media posts, can enhance trust.

Consumers often trust the opinions of their peers more than traditional advertising, and positive user-generated content can serve as powerful endorsements.

Influencer Marketing

1. **Credibility and Relatability**: Social media influencers can significantly impact consumer trust. Influencers who align with a brand's values and have a genuine connection with their audience can lend credibility and relatability to the brand. Their endorsements can make products and services more appealing to their followers.

2. **Engagement and Interaction**: Influencers often engage with their followers through comments, live sessions, and direct messages. This interaction fosters a sense of community and trust, as consumers feel they are part of a conversation rather than being targeted by impersonal advertisements.

Social Proof

1. **Reviews and Ratings**: Social media platforms provide a space for consumers to share their experiences through reviews and ratings. Positive reviews and high ratings can act as social proof, reassuring potential customers about the quality and reliability of a product or service.

2. **Recommendations and Shares**: When consumers see their friends and family recommending or sharing a brand's content, it can significantly boost trust. Social media's viral nature means that positive experiences can quickly spread, influencing a broader audience.

Transparency in Advertising

1. **Clear Disclosure**: Social media platforms have guidelines for disclosing sponsored content. Clear disclosure of paid partnerships and advertisements helps maintain transparency and trust. Consumers appreciate knowing when content is sponsored, as it allows them to make informed decisions.

2. **Authentic Content**: Brands that create authentic and engaging content, even in sponsored posts, can build trust. Consumers are more likely to trust content that feels genuine and aligns with their interests and values.

Crisis Management

1. **Real-Time Response**: Social media enables brands to respond to crises in real-time. Addressing issues promptly and transparently can mitigate damage and rebuild trust. Consumers appreciate when brands take responsibility and communicate openly during challenging times.

2. **Community Support**: During crises, brands can leverage social media to show support for their community. Whether it's through charitable initiatives, informative updates, or empathetic messaging, these actions can strengthen consumer trust and loyalty.

In summary, social media is a powerful tool for building and maintaining consumer trust. Through direct communication, influencer marketing, social proof, transparent advertising, and effective crisis management, brands can foster a trustworthy relationship with their audience

How to Handle Children's data

Handling children's data in the US involves navigating several privacy protection laws and best practices. The primary federal law is the Children's Online Privacy Protection Act (COPPA), which imposes requirements on websites and online services directed at children under 13 years of age. However, there are gaps in privacy protection that need to be addressed:

Key Gaps in Privacy Protection

1. **State-Level Variations:** While COPPA provides a federal framework, states like California have additional laws, such as the California Consumer Privacy Act (CCPA), which offer more stringent protections.

2. **Age Verification Challenges:** Ensuring accurate age verification can be difficult, leading to potential non-compliance and data breaches.

3. **Parental Consent:** Obtaining verifiable parental consent is crucial but can be complex and inconsistent across different platforms.

Best Practices for Handling Children's Data

1. **Conduct Youth Impact Assessments:** Regularly assess the risks associated with collecting and using children's data to develop appropriate safeguards.

2. **Implement High Privacy Settings by Default:** Ensure privacy settings are set to high by default for minors to protect their data.

3. **Clear and Child-Friendly Privacy Notices:** Use simple language and visuals to make privacy notices understandable for children.

4. **Age Verification Mechanisms:** Develop robust age verification processes to ensure compliance with laws like COPPA.

5. **Minimize Data Collection:** Collect only the data necessary for the intended purpose and avoid excessive data retention

When considering the application of the General Data Protection Regulation (GDPR) in the context of children's data in the US, several additional gaps in privacy protection become evident:

Additional Gaps in Privacy Protection

1. **Lack of Comprehensive Federal Law:** Unlike the GDPR, which provides a unified framework

across the EU, the US lacks a comprehensive federal privacy law that covers all aspects of data protection, including children's data.

2. **Inconsistent Age of Consent:** The GDPR sets the age of consent for data processing at 16, with the option for member states to lower it to 13. In the US, COPPA applies to children under 13, creating inconsistencies in age thresholds for data protection.
3. **Parental Consent Mechanisms:** The GDPR requires explicit consent from parents or guardians for processing children's data, with stringent verification processes. In contrast, COPPA's mechanisms for obtaining parental consent can be less rigorous.
4. **Data Minimization and Purpose Limitation:** The GDPR emphasizes data minimization and purpose limitation, ensuring that only necessary data is collected and used for specific purposes. US laws like COPPA do not always enforce these principles as strictly.
5. **Right to Erasure:** The GDPR grants individuals, including children, the right to have their data erased under certain conditions. This right is not as clearly defined or enforced under US laws.
6. **Profiling and Automated Decision-Making:** The GDPR places strict limitations on profiling and automated decision-making involving children's data. US regulations do not provide equivalent protections.

Enhancing Privacy Protection

To bridge these gaps, the US could consider adopting some of the GDPR's robust provisions, such as:

- **Unified Federal Privacy Law:** Implementing a comprehensive federal privacy law that aligns with GDPR principles.
- **Stricter Consent Requirements:** Enhancing mechanisms for obtaining and verifying parental consent.
- **Data Minimization:** Enforcing stricter data minimization and purpose limitation principles.
- **Enhanced Rights:** Providing children with clearer rights to access, correct, and erase their data.

By addressing these gaps, the US can improve the protection of children's data and align more closely with international standards.

Parents play a crucial role in protecting their children's data. Here are some practical steps and best practices to help ensure their privacy and safety online:

Best Practices for Parents

1. **Educate Your Children:** Teach your children about the importance of privacy and the risks of sharing personal information online. Encourage them to ask for permission before sharing any data.
2. **Use Parental Controls:** Utilize parental control features on devices and apps to monitor and restrict your children's online activities.

This can help prevent them from accessing inappropriate content and sharing personal information.

3. **Review Privacy Settings:** Regularly check and adjust the privacy settings on your children's devices, apps, and social media accounts to ensure their data is protected.
4. **Limit Data Sharing:** Encourage your children to share minimal personal information online. For example, they should avoid sharing their full name, address, phone number, or school name.
5. **Monitor App Permissions:** Review the permissions requested by apps before allowing your children to use them. Ensure that apps do not request unnecessary access to personal data.
6. **Use Secure Passwords:** Help your children create strong, unique passwords for their online accounts and teach them the importance of not sharing passwords with others.
7. **Stay Informed:** Keep up-to-date with the latest privacy laws and guidelines, such as COPPA and GDPR, to understand your rights and responsibilities as a parent.

Legal Guidelines

1. **COPPA Compliance:** Ensure that websites and online services your children use comply with the Children's Online Privacy Protection Act (COPPA). This law requires verifiable parental

consent before collecting personal information from children under 13.

2. **Review Privacy Policies:** Check the privacy policies of websites and apps to understand how they collect, use, and protect your children's data. Look for clear explanations and opt-out options.

3. **Exercise Your Rights:** Under COPPA, you have the right to review and delete your children's personal information collected by websites and services. Make use of these rights to manage your children's data effectively.

By following these steps, parents can better safeguard their children's privacy and help them navigate the digital world safely.

Part 5: GDPR in the Age of Artificial Intelligence

GDPR in the Age of Artificial Intelligence

The intersection of the General Data Protection Regulation (GDPR) and Artificial Intelligence (AI) raises critical questions about privacy, ethics, and data protection. As AI becomes increasingly central to innovation, GDPR is expected to evolve to address transparency, fairness, and accountability in AI-driven decision-making. One key area of change is explainability, as AI algorithms often function as "black boxes," making it difficult for users to understand how decisions are made. GDPR may require organizations to provide clear explanations of AI processes, particularly for high-impact decisions such as credit scoring and job applications. Businesses might also need to conduct algorithmic audits to ensure compliance with fairness and transparency standards.

Another evolving aspect is GDPR's stance on automated decision-making. Article 22 of GDPR grants individuals the right not to be subjected to decisions made solely by automated means without human intervention. This provision may be reinforced to require explicit consent before AI-driven decisions are applied in critical areas like hiring and finance. However, exceptions for AI in beneficial applications, such as healthcare diagnostics, may be introduced to balance innovation with privacy protections.

Bias in AI is another pressing concern, as models trained on large datasets can inadvertently reinforce discrimination. To address this, GDPR could introduce bias audits and fairness principles requiring organizations to evaluate and mitigate biases in AI models. Additionally, AI systems often rely on vast amounts of data, some of which is inferred rather than directly collected. GDPR may refine its consent mechanisms to introduce dynamic consent models, allowing users to adjust their preferences as AI systems evolve, and granular consent frameworks, enabling individuals to approve specific AI applications.

The principle of data minimization under GDPR, which mandates using only necessary data for specific purposes, presents challenges for AI, which thrives on large datasets. Future regulations may encourage the use of synthetic data to train AI models while reducing reliance on personal information. Similarly, adjustments to purpose limitation rules may be considered to foster AI development while maintaining data protection safeguards.

The EU AI Act, currently in development, classifies AI systems based on risk levels, complementing GDPR by establishing additional requirements for high-risk AI applications. GDPR may adapt by mandating additional Data Protection Impact Assessments (DPIAs) for AI systems processing personal data and ensuring alignment between GDPR and AI regulations.

Cross-border data transfers are another critical issue for AI development. Since AI models often require large-scale data flows across jurisdictions, GDPR may refine rules regarding international data transfers to ensure compliance with EU standards. Stricter mechanisms may be enforced for AI systems trained outside the EU to maintain privacy protections, and data localization requirements could be encouraged for high-risk AI applications.

Data Protection Authorities (DPAs) may gain more resources and tools to oversee AI-related data processing, issuing AI-specific guidelines and conducting proactive compliance checks, including model testing and algorithm reviews. Additionally, GDPR may introduce new rights for individuals, such as the right to algorithmic explanation, which would require AI-driven decisions to be interpretable. The right to data provenance could allow individuals to trace the origin of their data used in AI training, and the right to opt-out of AI-based profiling or automated decision-making could be strengthened.

Determining accountability for AI-related GDPR violations is another challenge. Regulations may introduce shared liability models, ensuring AI developers, providers, and users bear responsibility for compliance. Mandatory logging of AI decision-making processes may also be required to enhance transparency and accountability.

The rise of generative AI tools, such as ChatGPT and AI-driven image generators, introduces unique compliance concerns. GDPR may require organizations to disclose whether personal data was used in training generative AI models and expand the right to erasure to include data embedded in training datasets. As AI governance frameworks emerge globally, GDPR's principles are likely to influence international AI regulations, aligning with ethical guidelines like UNESCO's AI Ethics Recommendation and the OECD AI Principles.

While GDPR provides a robust foundation for AI governance, several challenges remain. Over-regulation could stifle AI innovation, while lenient rules might compromise privacy and fairness. Regulators will need technical expertise to evaluate complex AI models effectively, and efforts to harmonize GDPR with other regulatory frameworks, such as the U.S. AI Bill of Rights and China's AI policies, will be crucial.

Industry-Specific Impact of GDPR on AI

The influence of GDPR on AI applications varies across industries. In healthcare and biotech, AI-driven diagnostics and personalized medicine require balancing GDPR's data minimization principles with AI's need for extensive datasets. Explicit consent is essential for processing sensitive health data, and research projects may require anonymization or re-consent. Financial services must comply with GDPR's restrictions on AI-driven profiling and automated decision-making, ensuring explainability in credit scoring and fraud detection algorithms while preventing discriminatory outcomes.

In retail and e-commerce, AI-driven recommendation engines rely on behavioral tracking, necessitating explicit opt-in consent under GDPR. Customers retain the right to object to profiling, which can impact personalized marketing strategies. Social media and technology platforms must clarify how AI curates' content and moderates' posts, requiring transparent user notices and consent for AI-driven features.

Manufacturing and supply chain industries must ensure AI-powered workplace monitoring systems respect employee privacy rights, while organizations processing supply chain data across borders must comply with GDPR's international data transfer requirements. In education, AI-driven adaptive learning platforms processing student data must incorporate parental consent mechanisms and allow students to contest AI-driven grading decisions.

AI in transportation, particularly autonomous vehicles and mobility solutions, presents additional privacy challenges, as IoT-connected systems process location and sensor data. GDPR mandates explicit consent for location tracking, and companies deploying AI in self-driving technology must address liability concerns in case of privacy violations. Marketing and advertising agencies utilizing AI-driven programmatic advertising must ensure compliance with GDPR's consent requirements for tracking cookies and behavioral profiling, while gaming and entertainment platforms processing youth data must provide robust parental controls.

AI-driven HR and recruitment platforms processing applicant data must adhere to GDPR's transparency requirements, providing candidates with explanations for automated hiring decisions.

Organizations must also take proactive measures to prevent bias in AI-driven recruitment and workforce analytics.

Opportunities and Challenges for Businesses

While GDPR introduces compliance challenges, it also creates opportunities. Businesses that prioritize GDPR compliance in AI development can enhance trust among privacy-conscious consumers and differentiate themselves as leaders in ethical AI practices. Cross-industry collaboration in GDPR-compliant data handling fosters interoperability and innovation. However, ensuring compliance with GDPR's AI-related provisions requires significant resources, legal expertise, and technical infrastructure. Companies failing to comply risk substantial penalties, particularly in industries handling sensitive personal data, such as healthcare and finance.

Conclusion

As AI continues to evolve, GDPR must adapt to address emerging challenges in transparency, bias mitigation, accountability, and cross-border data flows. The regulation's evolution will aim to balance privacy protections with technological progress, ensuring AI remains ethical, fair, and accountable. Businesses leveraging AI must integrate GDPR principles into their compliance strategies to safeguard data privacy, build consumer trust, and navigate the complex regulatory landscape. By proactively aligning AI development with GDPR requirements, organizations can foster responsible innovation while maintaining data protection standards in the age of artificial intelligence.

GDPR Meets AI

Chapter 10:
GDPR Meets AI

Scenario 1: Your Smart Assistant Knows Too Much

Imagine you're in your kitchen, cooking, when your voice assistant, like Alexa or Google, suggests a recipe you'd love based on your previous requests. It feels like magic, but it's really AI at work, analyzing your voice commands and habits to serve you personalized recommendations.

Before GDPR: Without GDPR, smart assistants could collect data about your voice, location, and even purchases without explicit consent. This means your data could be shared, sold, or used for targeted ads without your knowledge.

Under GDPR: Now, under GDPR, companies must get explicit consent before collecting your data. You can request to access and delete any personal data they have on you. Companies must be transparent about how they're using your data to improve AI recommendations and provide clear opt-out options.

How GDPR Protects You: GDPR forces companies like Amazon and Google to be upfront about data usage, giving you more control over your voice and personal information.

Scenario 2: AI-Powered Hiring Systems

You apply for a job using an online system powered by AI. The system scans your resume, analyzes keywords, and decides whether you're a good fit. But when you get the rejection email, you're left wondering, why did the AI reject me?

Before GDPR: Many companies use AI to assess resumes, often without transparency about how decisions are made. AI systems could have biases, and you wouldn't necessarily know why you were rejected.

Under GDPR: GDPR demands transparency about how AI tools are evaluating your application. You have the right to explanation, meaning you can ask for a breakdown of how your resume was assessed and why you were rejected. AI cannot unfairly reject applicants based on personal factors like gender, race, or age.

How GDPR Protects You: If an AI decides about your job application, you can ask the employer to explain how it arrived at that conclusion. It ensures fairness and transparency.

Scenario 3: Personalized Content on Social Media

You open Facebook or Instagram, and the posts you see are incredibly tailored to your interests. Why? Because AI is analyzing your past likes, comments, and shares to predict what content you'll engage with next.

Before GDPR: Social media platforms track your interactions without asking for permission. Your personal data could be used to target you with ads or even shared with third-party companies without your knowledge.

Under GDPR: Explicit consent is required to collect and use your personal data. Transparency is key; you'll know how AI is shaping your feed and why you see certain posts. You can request all data stored on you by a platform and ask for it to be deleted. You also have the option to opt-out of personalized content and targeted ads.

How GDPR Protects You: GDPR gives you more control over how social media platforms use your data for AI-driven recommendations, allowing you to choose what you want to share and see.

AI Meets GDPR: Data Privacy in the Age of AI

The intersection of AI and GDPR presents a complex landscape where data privacy, transparency, and accountability are more important than ever. AI-driven technologies have become deeply integrated into daily life, from voice assistants and hiring systems to personalized content on social media. While these advancements offer convenience and efficiency, they also raise concerns about how personal data is collected, stored, and used. GDPR plays a critical role in ensuring that AI respects privacy rights and operates within ethical boundaries.

AI-powered voice assistants, such as Alexa and Google Assistant, process user commands to provide tailored recommendations. Before GDPR, these smart assistants could collect data on voice interactions, locations, and purchasing behavior without explicit consent. Users had limited visibility into how their data was being used or shared. Under GDPR, companies are now required to obtain explicit consent before collecting and processing user data. Individuals have the right to access and delete their stored personal data, ensuring greater control over their interactions with AI. Companies must also be transparent about how AI systems use collected data to enhance recommendations and must provide clear opt-out options for users who prefer not to share their information.

AI-driven hiring systems are another area where GDPR has significantly impacted data privacy. Many organizations use AI to scan resumes, analyze keywords, and make hiring decisions. Before GDPR, these systems often operated without transparency, making it difficult for job applicants to understand how decisions were made or to challenge rejections. GDPR now mandates that companies using AI for hiring must explain how their decision-making algorithms work. Applicants have the right to request information about how their resumes were assessed and why they were rejected. Moreover, AI-driven hiring tools must comply with non-discrimination principles, ensuring that biases related to gender, race, or age do not unfairly influence hiring outcomes. These protections make the recruitment process more transparent and equitable.

Social media platforms use AI to personalize user feeds based on past interactions, likes, and comments.

Before GDPR, these platforms could track user activity without permission, leveraging personal data for targeted advertising and third-party sharing without the user's knowledge. Under GDPR, explicit consent is required before social media companies can collect or process user data for AI-driven content recommendations. Users must be informed about how AI shapes their content feeds and why certain posts appear. Additionally, GDPR grants individuals the right to access, review, and delete stored personal data while offering opt-out options for personalized content and targeted ads. These measures provide users with greater control over their digital footprint and help protect against unwanted data exploitation.

As AI technologies continue to advance, GDPR plays a crucial role in regulating data privacy and security. AI systems thrive on large datasets, but GDPR emphasizes data minimization, ensuring that only necessary personal information is collected and retained. Transparency is a core principle of GDPR, requiring companies to explain how AI-driven decisions are made, whether in hiring, finance, or healthcare. Individuals have the right to challenge automated decisions, ensuring fairness and accountability in AI applications. The regulation also holds organizations accountable for AI errors and biases, requiring them to implement safeguards to protect user rights.

A significant concern surrounding AI is its impact on global privacy. Studies show that most people worry about AI misusing personal data, making biased decisions, or failing to explain its reasoning. GDPR addresses these concerns by enforcing the right to explanation and the right to access, making AI systems more transparent and user-friendly. This regulatory framework ensures that AI operates ethically and that individuals remain in control of their personal data.

Looking ahead, AI and GDPR must work together to foster responsible innovation. By enforcing strict data protection measures, GDPR encourages the development of privacy-conscious AI systems that respect individual rights. Ethical AI development, guided by GDPR, ensures fairness, accountability, and consumer trust. AI companies must balance innovation with regulatory compliance, integrating GDPR principles into their AI strategies to mitigate privacy risks.

In conclusion, AI is transforming industries by enhancing efficiency and personalization, but it also introduces privacy challenges that require strict regulatory oversight. GDPR ensures that AI respects data privacy and consumer rights by mandating transparency, accountability, and user control. Whether in voice assistants, hiring algorithms, or social media recommendations, individuals now have greater power to manage their personal data and challenge AI-driven decisions. As AI continues to evolve, GDPR will remain a fundamental safeguard, ensuring that privacy and technological progress go hand in hand.

Chapter II: Steps for U.S. Organizations to Align with GDPR

Practical Steps for U.S. Organizations to Align with GDPR

Understanding GDPR

Imagine you're at home with your family, browsing the internet, shopping for groceries online, or booking a doctor's appointment. Every time you enter your name, email, or credit card info, you're sharing personal data. But just like you wouldn't invite a stranger into your home without knowing what they're doing, your personal data should be treated with the same care—protected and respected.

GDPR is a set of rules designed to protect personal data and privacy in the European Union. But here's the catch: If your business collects personal data from people in the EU, you need to follow GDPR—even if your business is based in the U.S. Let's explore practical steps you can take to comply with GDPR.

Step 1: Know What Data You're Collecting

Scenario: Mom and Her Favorite Online Store

Imagine you're a mom who loves shopping online. You visit your favorite store's website, sign up for their newsletter, and enter your email and home address for delivery. You trust the company with your personal information, but how do you know they're protecting it properly?

What should the company do?

The company needs to know exactly what information they're collecting from you. They must also explain how they're using your information and why they need it. It could be to process your order, send you updates, or make recommendations based on your previous purchases.

Practical Action for Businesses:

Conduct a data audit: Look at every form on your website or app where people input personal data (email, address, payment info). Ask yourself:

- What data am I collecting?
- Why am I collecting this data?
- How long will I store it?

Simple Table: Types of Data U.S. Businesses Might Collect

Type of Data	Purpose	GDPR Requirement
Name & Email	Sending newsletters, updates, offers	Must get explicit consent from users
Credit Card Number	Processing payments	Must be securely stored and encrypted

Type of Data	Purpose	GDPR Requirement
Medical Information	Health tracking apps, insurance forms	Special care for sensitive data; explicit consent
IP Address	Website tracking, ads, and security	Users must be informed about data use

Additional Example: A small online boutique collects customer names, addresses, and purchase histories to personalize shopping experiences. They conduct a data audit and realize they also collect IP addresses for security purposes. They update their privacy policy to inform customers about this and ensure they have explicit consent for all data collected.

Step 2: Be Transparent and Ask for Consent

Scenario: The Local Doctor's Office

Let's say you're at a doctor's office. You fill out a form with your name, birthdate, and medical history. Before the receptionist hands you the form, they ask, "Are you okay with us using your information for appointment reminders and medical updates?"

What should happen?

Under GDPR, the doctor's office must ask for your permission to use your personal data for any specific purposes. It's not enough for them to just collect it—they must ask you clearly for your consent, especially if they want to use your info for marketing or sharing it with third-party partners.

Practical Action for Businesses:

- Get clear consent from customers before collecting data. Don't just assume you have it—ask for it.
- Make sure your privacy policy is clear, so customers know what's happening with their data.

Example: Clear Consent in Action

- Before GDPR: A pop-up might just say, "We collect your data."
- After GDPR: A pop-up should say, "By clicking 'Agree', you allow us to collect your email to send you order updates, promotions, and recommendations."

Additional Example: An online subscription service for meal kits updates its sign-up process to include a clear consent form. The form explains how customer data will be used for personalized meal recommendations and marketing emails. Customers must check a box to agree before proceeding.

Step 3: Keep Personal Data Safe

Scenario: Your Favorite Grocery Store App

Imagine you're using an app to order groceries online. You enter your address and payment details, trusting the store with your information. What happens if the grocery store's system gets hacked and your data is exposed?

What should the grocery store do?

GDPR mandates that businesses must protect your data. They can't just store your credit card number on a whim—they need to encrypt it to keep it safe from hackers.

Practical Action for Businesses:

- Encrypt sensitive data: Make sure any personal data (like credit card details, Social Security numbers, or health info) is encrypted, so it's unreadable to anyone who might intercept it.
- Limit access: Only authorized employees should have access to personal data. Think of it like locking up valuables in a safe—don't leave your data accessible to anyone who doesn't need it.

Additional Example: A financial services company implements encryption for all customer data, including bank account numbers and transaction histories. They also restrict access to this data to only a few key employees who need it for their work.

Step 4: Appoint a Data Protection Officer (DPO)

Scenario: The Big Corporation You Work For

You work for a company with thousands of employees and customers, handling sensitive information every day. Who's responsible for making sure your company follows GDPR and protects customers' data?

What should your company do?

If you process a lot of sensitive data (like health records or payment info), GDPR suggests appointing a Data Protection Officer (DPO). This person makes sure that your company follows all the privacy rules and is responsible for handling customer data requests.

Practical Action for Businesses:

If you run a large business or store sensitive data, hire or appoint a DPO who can ensure your organization complies with GDPR and is up to date with the latest regulations.

Additional Example: A multinational healthcare provider appoints a DPO to oversee data protection practices across all its locations. The DPO conducts regular training sessions for employees on GDPR compliance and handles any data-related inquiries from customers.

Step 5: Respect Data Subject Rights (Your Rights as a Consumer)

Scenario: The Mom with an Email Newsletter

You've been getting weekly email updates from a store you signed up for months ago. One day, you decide you don't want to receive any more emails. But how do you stop them?

What should the store do?

Under GDPR, you have the right to be forgotten. That means you can ask any business to delete your personal data or stop sending you messages. Businesses need to respect your wishes within a reasonable time frame.

Practical Action for Businesses:

- Honor opt-outs: If a customer wants to stop receiving emails, make sure it's easy for them to unsubscribe.
- Right to Access: Customers can ask to see the data you have on them. If they do, you need to provide it in a simple, readable format.

Additional Example: An online retailer includes an easy-to-find "unsubscribe" link in all marketing emails. When a customer clicks the link, they are immediately removed from the mailing list, and their data is deleted from the marketing database.

Step 6: Handle Data Breaches the Right Way

Scenario: Data Breach at the Local Retailer

Let's say a local store has a data breach. Hackers steal your credit card information from their website. You find out and panic. What should the store have done?

What should the store do?

GDPR says that businesses need to notify both customers and regulators within 72 hours if a data breach happens and there's a risk to your privacy. So, if your personal information is exposed, the store should reach out to you immediately and tell you what happened.

Practical Action for Businesses:

Have a data breach plan in place. If a breach happens, you need a quick way to notify customers and take steps to secure the information.

Real-World Fact:

In 2020, British Airways was fined $22 million for a data breach that exposed the personal details of over 400,000 customers (about half the population of Delaware). GDPR's penalties can be huge, so it's important to be prepared.

Additional Example: A small tech company experiences a data breach and immediately activates its data breach response plan. Within 24 hours, they notify affected customers and provide steps to secure their accounts, such as changing passwords and monitoring for suspicious activity.

Step 7: Keep Your Policies Updated

Scenario: Your Favorite Health App

You've been using a health app to track your exercise and eating habits. The company behind the app occasionally updates its terms of service and privacy policy. But how do you know if they're following the latest rules?

What should the app company do?

Under GDPR, businesses must keep their privacy policies up to date. They need to inform you if anything changes, like how your data is used or shared. If they start using your data for new purposes, they need to ask for your consent again.

Practical Action for Businesses:

- Review policies regularly: Set up regular reviews of your privacy policies to make sure they stay in line with current laws.

- Communicate changes: If anything changes, notify your customers immediately.

Additional Example: A fitness app updates its privacy policy to include new data-sharing practices with third-party health researchers. They notify all users via email and in-app notifications, asking for renewed consent to continue using the app under the new terms.

Key Steps to GDPR Compliance for U.S. Organizations

Ensuring compliance with GDPR requires U.S. organizations to adopt structured data protection practices. The first step is understanding what personal data is collected, how it is processed, and for what purpose. Conducting a thorough data audit helps organizations identify and categorize the personal information they store, ensuring that they collect only what is necessary and relevant. Once businesses understand their data flow, they must obtain clear and explicit consent from users before processing their information. Consent should be specific, informed, and easily withdrawable, with transparent explanations of how the data will be used.

Protecting personal data is equally critical. Businesses should implement robust security measures such as encryption, multi-factor authentication, and strict access controls to minimize the risk of breaches. Employee training plays a vital role in reinforcing these security measures, ensuring that staff can identify threats like phishing attacks and unauthorized data access. Larger organizations that process significant amounts of sensitive data may be required to appoint a Data Protection Officer (DPO) to oversee GDPR compliance, advise on data protection policies, and act as a point of contact for regulatory authorities.

Respecting consumer rights is another fundamental aspect of GDPR compliance. Individuals have the right to access their data, request corrections, and even demand its deletion under the "right to be forgotten." Organizations must establish efficient systems to handle these requests promptly and in compliance with GDPR timelines. Additionally, companies must have a well-defined data breach response plan. If a breach occurs, they are required to notify regulators within 72 hours and inform affected individuals if there is a risk to their personal data.

Maintaining compliance is not a one-time effort but an ongoing process. Organizations must regularly review and update their privacy policies, ensuring they align with evolving regulations and industry best practices. Any changes in data collection methods or processing activities must be communicated clearly to consumers, with renewed consent obtained when necessary. By proactively maintaining compliance, businesses can mitigate risks and demonstrate their commitment to data protection.

Small businesses often face challenges in GDPR compliance due to limited resources and technical expertise. Common pitfalls include weak password policies, lack of employee training, insufficient data backups, and failure to encrypt sensitive information. Many businesses neglect to update their software regularly, leaving systems vulnerable to cyberattacks. Poor access controls can expose personal data to unauthorized users, increasing the risk of breaches. Another common mistake is failing to dispose of data that is no longer needed, which can lead to excessive data retention and legal risks. Businesses must also be vigilant about recognizing and responding to subject access requests from individuals seeking to review or delete their data.

Cybersecurity awareness plays a crucial role in preventing data breaches. Employees should be trained to recognize suspicious emails, avoid clicking on unknown links, and verify the legitimacy of attachments before opening them. Neglecting regulatory obligations, such as failing to renew registration with the Information Commissioner's Office (ICO), can lead to unnecessary fines and compliance issues. By addressing these vulnerabilities and implementing best practices, small businesses can significantly strengthen their data protection strategies.

Conclusion: GDPR for U.S. Organizations is About Respecting Privacy

GDPR compliance is not just about avoiding fines—it is about respecting individuals' privacy rights and fostering trust with consumers. Businesses that prioritize data protection gain a competitive advantage by demonstrating their commitment to transparency and security. Adhering to GDPR principles ensures that personal data is handled ethically and responsibly, reinforcing consumer confidence in an increasingly data-driven world.

GDPR might seem like a complicated law designed for European businesses, but it has a **big impact** on U.S. companies that deal with personal data from EU citizens. By following these practical steps—understanding the data you collect, protecting it, and respecting people's privacy—you build trust with customers, protect your business, and avoid penalties.

It's just like protecting your family's information: You wouldn't let a stranger have access to your child's school records without asking first, right?

In the same way, GDPR ensures that businesses treat **your personal data** with respect. Just as individuals take precautions to safeguard their personal information at home, organizations must uphold the same level of diligence in managing the data entrusted to them.

Part 6: Need for Change of Work Culture

Bring the change

Bringing change through the implementation of GDPR principles in daily business operations fosters a culture of data protection, trust, and regulatory compliance. To effectively integrate GDPR into business practices, the process must start with building awareness and securing leadership commitment.

Educating employees through workshops and training sessions ensures that teams understand the significance of data protection, while leadership buy-in ensures that adequate resources and attention are allocated to privacy initiatives. A top-down approach helps establish a corporate culture where data privacy is a core priority.

Conducting a comprehensive data audit is a crucial next step. Businesses must map their data flows to identify what personal information they collect, where it is stored, and how it is processed. This audit helps assess compliance risks, ensuring that data processing aligns with GDPR principles such as data minimization. Keeping records of these data processing activities, as required under Article 30 of GDPR, ensures that businesses can demonstrate accountability and transparency.

Updating policies and procedures is necessary to align with GDPR's requirements. Privacy policies must be revised to ensure they are transparent, easy to understand, and clearly outline data collection and usage practices. Consent mechanisms should be refined to ensure explicit, informed, and easily revocable consent from users. Additionally, businesses must establish efficient workflows to handle data subject requests, including access, deletion, and rectification requests, to ensure compliance with GDPR's user rights.

Embedding privacy by design is essential in developing GDPR-compliant business processes. This means integrating privacy considerations into all new projects and systems from the outset. Organizations should default to collecting the minimum amount of personal data necessary for a given purpose and should employ techniques such as anonymization and pseudonymization to reduce the risk of exposing personally identifiable information.

Data security measures must be strengthened to protect sensitive personal information. Implementing access controls ensures that only authorized personnel can access personal data, reducing the likelihood of unauthorized exposure. Encryption protects sensitive data both during storage and transmission. Additionally, businesses must develop and maintain a well-defined incident response plan to quickly detect, report, and mitigate the impact of data breaches, ensuring compliance with GDPR's 72-hour breach notification requirement.

Designating key roles within the organization enhances GDPR compliance. Businesses handling significant amounts of personal data may need to appoint a Data Protection Officer (DPO) to oversee data protection strategies and compliance efforts. Even if a DPO is not legally required, designating privacy ambassadors within key departments can help reinforce data protection practices across the organization.

Regular employee training is essential to ensure that staff members understand their role in protecting personal data. Training should include practical, real-world scenarios to help employees recognize potential risks, such as phishing attacks or improper data sharing. Ongoing education fosters a privacy-conscious workforce that proactively upholds GDPR principles.

Strengthening relationships with vendors and partners is equally important, as third parties often process personal data on behalf of businesses. Organizations must update data processing agreements to ensure vendors adhere to GDPR standards. Conducting due diligence on vendors' data protection practices helps mitigate risks associated with third-party data handling, and ongoing monitoring ensures continued compliance.

Respecting data subject rights is a fundamental GDPR requirement. Businesses must have systems in place to respond promptly to access requests, allowing individuals to obtain a copy of their data. Mechanisms for data deletion and rectification must be streamlined to allow individuals to correct inaccuracies or request data erasure. Opt-out options should be easily accessible, giving consumers control over their participation in data processing activities, such as marketing communications.

Promoting transparency enhances customer trust and regulatory compliance. Open communication about data collection and processing practices reassures consumers about how their information is handled. User-friendly tools, such as preference management interfaces, allow individuals to control their data-sharing preferences easily. Demonstrating GDPR compliance can serve as a competitive advantage, reinforcing brand trust and customer loyalty.

Ongoing monitoring and continuous improvement are essential to maintaining GDPR compliance. Regular audits help identify areas for improvement, ensuring that data protection practices remain effective and up to date. Organizations must stay informed about evolving GDPR regulations and interpretations, adapting their policies as necessary. Feedback from audits, regulatory updates, and stakeholder input should be used to refine privacy strategies.

Benefits of Implementing GDPR in Daily Business Life

The benefits of implementing GDPR in daily business operations extend beyond compliance. Prioritizing data protection fosters customer trust, making consumers more likely to engage with businesses that demonstrate responsible data handling. GDPR compliance reduces legal and financial risks, helping organizations avoid fines and reputational damage resulting from data breaches. Additionally, implementing structured data management practices enhances operational efficiency. Aligning with GDPR principles also prepares businesses for global markets, positioning them competitively in jurisdictions with strict data protection regulations.

By embedding GDPR principles into everyday business processes, companies can establish a sustainable data privacy framework that benefits both the organization and its stakeholders. This proactive approach not only ensures compliance but also reinforces ethical business practices, fostering a more secure and transparent digital landscape.

Chapter 12: Creating a Culture of Security

Creating a culture of data security in companies

Creating a culture of data security within a small business is essential for safeguarding sensitive information, fostering customer trust, and ensuring compliance with regulatory requirements. Achieving this goal requires a structured approach that integrates leadership commitment, employee training, and the implementation of strong security measures into everyday business operations.

Leadership plays a critical role in establishing a security-first mindset. Business leaders must set the tone by prioritizing data protection and allocating resources for necessary security initiatives. They should communicate the importance of cybersecurity across all levels, reinforcing that data security is a shared responsibility, not just an IT concern. By demonstrating their commitment, leaders encourage employees to adopt best practices and take security seriously.

Developing comprehensive data security policies is the next step in embedding a culture of security. These policies should outline how employees should handle, store, and transfer data, clearly defining roles and responsibilities at various levels. When employees understand their accountability, they are more likely to follow established protocols, reducing the risk of security breaches.

Developing comprehensive data security policies are fundamental to securing company data. Employees should be required to use complex, unique passwords for their accounts, supported by multi-factor authentication (MFA) to prevent unauthorized access. Additionally, businesses should enforce the principle of least privilege, ensuring that employees have access only to the data necessary for their roles. By limiting data exposure, companies can significantly reduce the risk of internal threats and accidental leaks.

Regular employee training is essential for maintaining awareness of cybersecurity threats. Training sessions should cover phishing scams, password management, safe browsing habits, and best practices for handling sensitive data. Simulated phishing exercises can help employees recognize and respond to cyber threats, reinforcing their knowledge through real-world scenarios. Continuous education fosters a vigilant workforce that actively contributes to the company's security posture.

Data backups and encryption add another layer of protection. Businesses should schedule automated backups of critical data and store copies securely, either on encrypted cloud platforms or external storage devices. Encryption ensures that even if data is intercepted, it remains unreadable to unauthorized parties. Additionally, companies must install and update antivirus software to protect devices from malware, ensuring that all endpoints remain secure.

Proactive monitoring of systems for suspicious activity can help detect potential security threats before they escalate. Network monitoring tools can flag unusual activity, such as unauthorized data transfers or login attempts. Having an incident response plan in place ensures that employees know how to react swiftly to potential breaches, minimizing damage and mitigating risks.

Compliance with relevant data protection laws is crucial for avoiding legal and financial repercussions. Businesses must familiarize themselves with regulations such as GDPR, CCPA, or HIPAA, ensuring that their security policies align with legal requirements. Regular policy reviews and updates are necessary to adapt to evolving regulations and maintain compliance.

Open communication about security concerns helps create an environment where employees feel comfortable reporting potential threats without fear of blame. Establishing secure reporting channels and providing IT support resources allows employees to seek guidance when encountering security challenges.

A well-defined breach response plan is essential for minimizing the impact of data breaches. Businesses must establish clear protocols for containing breaches, investigating incidents, notifying affected individuals, and implementing recovery measures. Employees should be trained on these procedures to ensure a coordinated response in case of an emergency.

Ensuring that vendors and third-party partners adhere to security standards is another important aspect of data protection. Before entering agreements, businesses should evaluate the security practices of external providers and require data protection agreements when handling sensitive information. Ongoing monitoring of vendor compliance helps prevent potential security risks.

To promote a security-first mindset, businesses should integrate data security into their company culture. Employees should be encouraged to incorporate security considerations into their daily activities, from sending emails to managing files. Recognizing and rewarding employees who actively contribute to data security efforts fosters engagement and reinforces positive behaviors.

Conclusion

Building a strong data security culture requires a holistic approach that combines leadership commitment, clear policies, ongoing education, and technical safeguards. When every employee plays an active role in data protection, businesses can strengthen their security posture, protect sensitive information, and build long-term trust with customers and stakeholders. By embedding security into daily business operations, companies can create a sustainable framework that prioritizes data privacy and resilience against cyber threats.

Chapter 13: Initiatives for Security Culture

Security Culture Initiatives and How to Measure Their Impact

Creating a security culture within a small business is not just about implementing policies but also about fostering a mindset where everyone takes responsibility for data protection. Here are some real-world examples of successful security culture initiatives from small companies that effectively built a strong security-first mindset:

Buffer: Regular "Security Hygiene" Checks

Buffer, a small but rapidly growing social media management tool company, implemented a culture of continuous security awareness by performing regular "security hygiene" checks across the entire company. This included auditing employee access levels to various systems, ensuring employees adhered to strong password practices, and keeping all software up to date. They held monthly security meetings for the entire company, where they discussed current threats, reviewed past incidents, and conducted security drills. They also had an open-door policy where employees could ask questions or report concerns without judgment. This transparency and focus on proactive security measures helped Buffer stay on top of potential security risks while ensuring every team member felt responsible for the company's cybersecurity efforts.

Snyk: "Security Champions" Program

Snyk, a security software company for developers, implemented a "Security Champions" program, where they appointed employees across various departments to act as the first line of defense for security within their teams. These "champions" acted as go-to individuals for security advice, helping to build a peer-to-peer security culture. Security Champions were given specialized training and resources to help them address and educate their peers about best practices in securing code, managing vulnerabilities, and safeguarding personal data. They would also lead security discussions during team meetings and review new features or projects for security risks. By integrating security awareness into each department, Snyk cultivated a decentralized approach to security, where everyone in the company played a part in maintaining robust data protection. This fostered an atmosphere of shared responsibility and collective ownership of security.

Mailchimp: Integrating Security into Onboarding

Mailchimp, an email marketing platform, rooted its security culture in its onboarding process for new hires. From day one, employees are trained not only on their specific roles but also on the company's security policies and best practices. New hires undergo security orientation during their first week, which includes understanding Mailchimp's security infrastructure, the importance of safeguarding customer data, and how they can contribute to security measures in their specific roles. Employees are also taught to recognize and avoid phishing attempts and how to securely handle sensitive data. By embedding security awareness into the onboarding process, Mailchimp ensured that new employees were immediately aligned with the company's security standards. This practice has been successful in reducing security incidents and building a security-first mindset across the company.

Automattic: Encouraging "Security as a Habit"

Automattic, the creator of WordPress, fosters a culture where security is ingrained into daily operations, emphasizing that security is not an afterthought but something that should be built into every project from the beginning. The company promotes a security-first approach for all employees, with a focus on creating habits around security. For instance, developers are encouraged to think about security when writing code, and all employees use two-factor authentication (2FA) as part of their standard workflow. The company also provides ongoing training and security updates to keep staff aware of emerging threats. Automattic's approach to security as a habit has led to a more resilient environment, where security is second nature to employees. This proactive mindset minimizes the likelihood of vulnerabilities and allows the company to catch and resolve issues faster.

Basecamp: Cross-Team Collaboration for Data Protection

Basecamp, a project management software company, implemented a cross-team collaboration strategy, where security and IT teams worked closely with other departments such as HR, customer support, and marketing to ensure security was prioritized across all aspects of the business. Basecamp held regular cross-department security workshops where employees from all functions participated in discussions about potential security threats, practical steps for reducing risk, and methods to improve the company's overall security posture. Security was incorporated into every project and decision-making process. This cross-functional approach made security a shared responsibility among all teams, preventing security issues from being siloed within the IT department. The company benefited from employees at every level actively contributing to improving security practices, enhancing the overall safety of the business.

DuckDuckGo: Transparent Security Communication

DuckDuckGo, a privacy-focused search engine, created an environment of open communication about security. The company made it a point to ensure that employees, from engineers to customer support staff, were always informed about the latest security threats and changes to internal policies. DuckDuckGo hosted monthly security roundtables, where the security team would present updates on the latest vulnerabilities, ongoing projects, and any lessons learned from recent incidents. These meetings were open to all employees and served as an informal, yet effective way to promote transparency. As a privacy-focused company, DuckDuckGo ensured that security was central to its culture. These transparent communications helped employees stay vigilant about security risks and empowered them to identify and respond to threats proactively.

Shopify: Gamification of Security Awareness

Shopify, an e-commerce platform, used gamification to increase employee engagement in security training and awareness. The company implemented a platform where employees could complete security-related challenges and earn rewards for correctly identifying potential risks. Shopify created an interactive and competitive environment where employees competed in teams to complete tasks like spotting phishing emails, securing their accounts, or finding vulnerabilities in the system. The gamified process helped employees internalize security best practices in a fun and engaging way. This approach led to a significant increase in employee participation in security training and a more enthusiastic commitment to maintaining security protocols across the organization.

These examples show that building a **security-first culture** is not about imposing strict rules or relying solely on IT teams but about embedding security into every part of a company's operations. Whether through **ongoing training**, **cross-department collaboration**, **clear communication**, or innovative approaches like gamification, small businesses can effectively foster a culture of security. The key is to **empower employees**, encourage **transparency**, and make security an everyday priority, ensuring that every individual contributes to protecting sensitive data and company assets.

Measuring the impact of security culture initiatives is crucial for understanding whether the efforts are leading to meaningful changes in behavior, enhancing the overall security posture, and reducing the likelihood of security breaches. For small companies, it is especially important because resources are often limited, and ensuring the effectiveness of security initiatives helps prioritize investment and guide future efforts. Here's how you can measure the impact and why it matters:

Key Metrics to Measure the Impact of Security Culture Initiatives

Creating a robust security culture within a small business involves more than just implementing policies; it requires fostering a mindset where everyone takes responsibility for data protection. Here are some key metrics to measure the impact of security culture initiatives:

Employee Participation and Engagement: Track the level of engagement in training programs, workshops, and security-related events. This includes monitoring how many employees attend security meetings, complete online security courses, or participate in security simulations. High participation indicates that employees are engaged and taking ownership of security, suggesting that the company's messaging and training efforts are resonating. Conversely, low participation might indicate a lack of awareness or interest, signaling a need for improved engagement strategies.

Security Incident Frequency and Severity: Monitor the number and types of security incidents or breaches, such as phishing attempts, malware infections, data leaks, or unauthorized access. Track how many of these incidents are successfully detected and prevented due to employee vigilance. A reduction in incidents after launching security initiatives is a direct indicator that the culture shift is taking place, suggesting employees are better at identifying and mitigating risks, resulting in fewer data breaches or attacks.

Phishing Simulation Success Rate: Conduct regular phishing tests to see how many employees fall for phishing attempts. Over time, measure whether the percentage of employees who click on suspicious links decreases as training progresses. Phishing is one of the most common attack vectors for small businesses. A decrease in successful phishing attacks shows that employees are internalizing lessons and becoming more cautious when dealing with suspicious emails or communications.

Compliance with Security Policies and Procedures: Audit how well employees are adhering to established security protocols, such as password policies, data handling guidelines, and access control measures. You can use tools to automatically track compliance or conduct manual checks. Consistent adherence to security policies indicates that employees understand their responsibilities and are taking the necessary steps to protect sensitive data. If employees are not following the policies, it suggests a gap in understanding or enforcement.

Employee Feedback and Security Culture Surveys: Conduct regular surveys or feedback sessions to assess how employees feel about the company's security culture. Ask questions about their confidence in handling security risks, their awareness of policies, and whether they feel the company supports security efforts. Direct feedback helps gauge whether the security culture is being internalized and whether employees feel empowered to act on security concerns. It also reveals areas where employees may need additional support or training.

Time to Detection and Response to Security Incidents: Track the time it takes from when a security incident occurs to when it is detected and resolved. A faster detection and response time indicates that employees are more vigilant and proactive. Quick detection and response are crucial for minimizing the impact of security breaches. If employees can identify and address security threats faster, it reflects the effectiveness of the security culture.

Security Incident Costs and Impact: Measure the financial and operational impact of security Incidents, including fines, lost business, downtime, or legal costs. Compare costs before and after implementing security culture initiatives. A reduction in the cost of security incidents indicates that the company is better at preventing, detecting, and mitigating threats, thereby improving its bottom line. Small businesses often have limited resources, so preventing costly breaches is especially critical.

Retention and Satisfaction of Security-Specific Employees: Track retention rates of employees in roles like IT security or compliance. Conduct satisfaction surveys to understand how these employees feel about the company's commitment to security. If security professionals feel supported and valued, they are more likely to remain with the company, ensuring long-term security continuity. High turnover in security roles can be a sign that the culture needs improvement.

Why Measuring Security Culture is Crucial for Small Businesses

Resource Allocation: Small businesses typically have limited resources. Measuring the effectiveness of security initiatives allows you to allocate resources where they are most needed. If certain initiatives are more successful than others, you can prioritize and refine those efforts.

Demonstrating ROI on Security Investments: Many small businesses struggle to justify investments in cybersecurity. By measuring the impact of security culture initiatives, you can demonstrate the return on investment for security programs. If security initiatives lead to fewer incidents, reduced downtime, or less expensive data breaches, you can justify continued or increased investments in security.

Regulatory Compliance: Small businesses are often subject to data protection regulations like GDPR, CCPA, or HIPAA. Measuring the effectiveness of security initiatives helps ensure that your company remains compliant with these regulations and avoids potential fines or legal action. A strong security culture ensures that employees understand and follow the rules, minimizing the risk of non-compliance.

Continuous Improvement: The threat landscape evolves constantly, and small businesses need to adapt. By regularly measuring and assessing the effectiveness of security culture initiatives, you can identify areas for improvement and make data-driven decisions to enhance the culture and tighten security controls.

Risk Management: Small businesses are often prime targets for cybercriminals because they tend to have weaker security measures. By fostering a culture of security and measuring its impact, small businesses can better manage risks and reduce the likelihood of a successful attack. The more vigilant and prepared employees are the less likely the company is to fall victim to a cyber-attack.

Building Trust with Customers and Partners: A company's reputation is a critical asset, and maintaining a strong security culture helps protect that reputation. Customers and partners want assurance that their data is safe. Demonstrating a strong security culture through clear policies, training, and good incident response builds trust and strengthens relationships.

Conclusion

For small businesses, measuring the impact of security culture initiatives is essential for improving security over time, ensuring that efforts align with business objectives, and reducing risk. By tracking participation, incidents, employee feedback, and financial impact, you can ensure that your security culture is not only a set of ideals but a tangible, impactful part of your daily operations. Small businesses that effectively measure and improve their security culture are better positioned to protect their data, comply with regulations, and build trust with customers.

Chapter 14:
Final Thought for U.S. Families and Individuals

While the General Data Protection Regulation (GDPR) is a European law, its global impact is significant, especially for families and individuals in the U.S. As technology and digital services increasingly cross borders, GDPR sets a high standard for data privacy and consumer protection, and its influence is felt in the U.S. as more companies and platforms are required to comply with its rules.

The Benefits of GDPR for Families and Individuals

For families and individuals, GDPR brings many important benefits. One of the most significant advantages is greater control over personal data. Whether it's related to online shopping, social media, or health apps, GDPR ensures that businesses must ask for your consent before collecting or using your data. This means you can opt out of tracking or delete your data whenever you choose, giving you more autonomy over your personal information.

Another key benefit is stronger privacy protections. GDPR provides higher levels of protection for sensitive data, such as health, financial, or location information. This is particularly critical as families increasingly engage with smart devices and apps in their daily lives. With GDPR, your personal information is safeguarded more rigorously, reducing the risk of misuse or unauthorized access.

Transparency and accountability are also central to GDPR. Whether it's an app, social media platform, or service provider, GDPR demands clear explanations of how your data is being used. Companies must be accountable for how they store, process, and secure your information, making it easier for you to understand and make informed decisions about your data.

For families in the U.S., GDPR represents a shift toward greater data rights, encouraging U.S.-based companies to adopt similar privacy practices. As more companies comply with GDPR's standards, you benefit from improved security and privacy controls without having to worry about the borders of the EU. This means that even outside the EU, you can enjoy the enhanced protections and greater control over your personal data that GDPR provides.

For families in the U.S., GDPR represents a shift toward greater data rights, encouraging U.S.-based companies to adopt similar privacy practices. As more companies comply with GDPR's standards, you benefit from improved security and privacy controls without having to worry about the borders of the EU.

Ultimately, GDPR serves as a reminder that privacy is a right, not a privilege, and that families and individuals should be empowered to protect their personal information. While compliance with GDPR is mostly on the companies, U.S. citizens are the true beneficiaries of its broader principles, making the digital world safer and more transparent for everyone.

As digital connectivity expands and artificial intelligence reshapes industries, the need to safeguard personal data has never been more urgent. The European Union's General Data Protection Regulation (GDPR) has emerged as a global benchmark for data privacy, setting rigorous standards that extend far beyond Europe's borders. While initially designed for EU citizens, GDPR's influence reaches U.S. businesses, consumers, and institutions, as personal data flows seamlessly across international networks. Whether shopping online, using social media, or interacting with digital healthcare systems, Americans are directly impacted by the regulation's principles, even when they are not explicitly aware of them.

Throughout this book, we have explored the fundamental pillars of GDPR, detailing the rights it grants individuals and the responsibilities it imposes on organizations. We have examined its implications for U.S. businesses, healthcare providers, and everyday consumers, illustrating how data protection is no longer an abstract legal concept but an essential component of modern digital life. Through real-world scenarios and practical compliance strategies, we have highlighted the importance of proactive data management and the evolving role of privacy in an AI-driven world.

The central takeaway is clear: data privacy is not just about compliance—it is about shaping a future where individuals have greater control over their personal information, businesses build trust through transparency, and emerging technologies operate within ethical boundaries. The way we approach data protection today will determine the security and privacy of future generations, making it essential to adopt policies and practices that uphold these principles in an increasingly digital world.

The Increasing Importance of Data Privacy

In today's digital landscape, individuals engage with numerous online platforms, whether for social networking, shopping, healthcare, or everyday transactions. Each interaction involves sharing personal information, often without a second thought. Yet, the fundamental questions remain: How much control do we truly have over our data? Can we trust that it is handled responsibly? And if our privacy is compromised, what options do we have for recourse?

The rise of artificial intelligence and data-driven technologies has amplified these concerns. AI systems process vast amounts of personal information rapidly, often in ways that are opaque to the user. While these advancements bring undeniable benefits—enhancing medical diagnostics, tailoring online experiences, and streamlining customer service—they also pose serious risks regarding privacy, accountability, and data security. The General Data Protection Regulation (GDPR) addresses these issues by establishing strict guidelines for how data is collected, stored, and used. More importantly, it empowers individuals by granting them rights over their personal information, ensuring transparency in data processing, and holding businesses accountable.

GDPR's Role in Daily Life

At the core of this discussion is a simple yet critical question: Why should GDPR matter to Americans? The reality is that, from the moment we go online each day, GDPR influences how companies handle our data. Whether it's a prompt asking for consent before tracking cookies, an option to unsubscribe from targeted ads, or the ability to request the deletion of stored information, these measures reflect the regulation's widespread impact—even in the U.S.

Although GDPR is primarily designed to protect EU citizens, its principles have set a global standard that businesses worldwide must consider. Concepts such as privacy by design, data minimization, and the right to be forgotten are increasingly becoming best practices, even for American companies. From healthcare providers safeguarding patient records to businesses ensuring transparency in their data policies, adopting GDPR-like protections is not just a legal necessity for companies operating internationally—it is also a step toward building trust and fostering responsible data management. As digital privacy continues to evolve, understanding and embracing these protections will be crucial for individuals and organizations alike.

Key Takeaways from This Book

1. **Individual Rights Matter**
2. **Healthcare and Personal Data**
3. **AI and the Future of Privacy**
4. **Practical Steps for Businesses**

The implementation of GDPR has fundamentally reshaped the way personal data is managed, emphasizing individual rights and placing responsibility on businesses to handle data ethically. One of the most significant takeaways is the empowerment of individuals to control their personal information. GDPR grants the right to access, modify, and even delete personal data, reinforcing the principle that privacy is not a privilege but a fundamental right. This shift not only benefits consumers but also establishes a global expectation for businesses to treat customer data with transparency and respect.

In the healthcare sector, where sensitive data is frequently collected and stored, the intersection of GDPR and existing U.S. laws like HIPAA presents new challenges. While HIPAA ensures confidentiality within the American healthcare system, GDPR introduces additional rights, such as data portability and the right to erasure. As healthcare systems become increasingly digitized, the need for harmonization between these regulations is growing, ensuring that patient privacy remains at the forefront of technological advancements.

The rise of artificial intelligence introduces another layer of complexity to data protection. AI systems rely on vast amounts of personal data to function, making transparency, accountability, and informed consent critical considerations. GDPR has set a precedent for requiring organizations to disclose how AI-driven decisions are made and how data is processed. As AI becomes more integrated into daily life, from personalized marketing to predictive healthcare, regulations like GDPR will continue to play a vital role in shaping ethical data practices.

For businesses, aligning with GDPR is not just about compliance—it is about fostering consumer trust. Companies that prioritize privacy by design, conduct data audits, secure clear consent, and safeguard customer information will gain a competitive advantage in a marketplace where consumers are more conscious of how their data is used. Implementing these best practices, as discussed in earlier chapters, ensures not only legal compliance but also strengthens customer relationships in an era where data protection is a growing concern.

The Future of Data Privacy

As digital interactions increase, the need for stronger privacy protections will only grow. GDPR has set a global benchmark, influencing regulations worldwide, including the California Consumer Privacy Act (CCPA). This shift signals a broader movement toward more stringent data privacy laws, and in the future, the U.S. may see the introduction of a nationwide privacy framework modeled after GDPR principles. As businesses, consumers, and lawmakers continue to push for greater control over personal data, we can expect an ongoing evolution of privacy laws to address emerging challenges posed by AI, machine learning, and advanced data analytics.

Beyond regulations, the responsibility of data protection extends to individuals, parents, and educators. Teaching younger generations about privacy, digital footprints, and responsible data sharing is essential in an age where personal information is constantly collected and analyzed. As society moves further into the digital era, fostering awareness and advocating for ethical data practices will be key to ensuring that privacy remains a protected right, not an afterthought. The future of data privacy depends on collective action—from policymakers to businesses to everyday users—to ensure that technological advancements align with fundamental human rights.

Conclusion

Privacy is a fundamental right that ensures individuals have control over their personal information and how it is shared. In today's digital age, where personal data is often collected, processed, and stored by companies and organizations, the importance of privacy has become even more critical. The General Data Protection Regulation (GDPR), a law enacted by the European Union, is designed to protect the privacy of individuals by setting strict guidelines on how personal data is handled. While the GDPR is an EU regulation, it can still benefit US citizens, particularly those whose data is handled by companies operating internationally. The GDPR empowers individuals by providing the right to access their data, request corrections, or even demand deletion of their personal information. For example, if a person realizes that their data is being used without consent or for purposes they didn't agree to, they can invoke their rights under the GDPR to request that their data be erased or corrected. Additionally, companies must provide clear and transparent information about how personal data is collected and used, ensuring that individuals are informed about their privacy rights.

GDPR enhances privacy in everyday life by giving individuals more control over their personal data and holding companies accountable for data protection. Here are some examples of how it helps:

1. **Right to Be Forgotten** – If you no longer want a company to store your personal data (such as an old social media account or an online shopping profile), you can request that they delete it entirely.
2. **Data Breach Notifications** – If a company suffers a data breach exposing your personal information, GDPR requires them to notify you quickly, allowing you to act (e.g., changing passwords or monitoring for fraud).
3. **Clear Consent for Data Use** – When signing up for a service, companies must explicitly ask for your consent to collect and use your data, preventing them from selling or sharing it without your knowledge.
4. **Access to Your Data** – You can request a copy of all the data a company has collected about you, giving you transparency and control over what information is stored.
5. **Opting Out of Tracking** – Many websites track users for targeted advertising. Under GDPR, you have the right to decline tracking cookies and prevent your data from being shared without consent.
6. **Protection Against Spam and Unwanted Marketing** – Companies must get clear permission

before sending marketing emails, reducing spam and unwanted solicitations.

Even though GDPR is an EU law, many global companies follow its rules, benefiting US citizens when dealing with international businesses or platforms that operate in Europe.

Index

www.ingramcontent.com/pod-product-compliance
Lightning Source LLC
LaVergne TN
LVHW090320210926
848480LV00001B/307

* 9 7 9 8 8 9 7 4 4 8 8 5 2 *